INDIAN COOKBOOK

Made Simple, at Home

The complete guide around India to the discovery of the tastiest traditional recipes such as homemade tandoori or butter chicken, naan, and much more

Chef MARINO

Chef Marino

Acknowledgment

I want to thank you for buying my book and for trusting in me, sincerely ...Thanks!

Writing a book is harder than I thought and more rewarding than I could have ever imagined.

My thanks go to all of you, readers, I thank you because without you I could not be what I am, without you my books simply...would not exist!

I would like to introduce you all my works, and, if you like them, invite you to leave a positive thought; this will help me to continue my work and will help other people to buy what they are looking for!

Again...Thanks You!

Chef Marino

Indian Cookbook

In this Series

Chef Marino

© Copyright 2021 by
All rights reserved.

This document is geared towards providing exact and reliable information with regard to the topic and issue covered. The publication is sold with the idea that the publisher is not required to render accounting, officially permitted, or otherwise, qualified services. If advice is necessary, legal or professional, a practiced individual in the profession should be ordered.

- From a Declaration of Principles which was accepted and approved equally by a Committee of the American Bar Association and a Committee of Publishers and Associations.

In no way is it legal to reproduce, duplicate, or transmit any part of this document in either electronic means or in printed format. Recording of this publication is strictly prohibited and any storage of this document is not allowed unless with written permission from the publisher. All rights reserved.

The information provided herein is stated to be truthful and consistent, in that any liability, in terms of inattention or otherwise, by any usage or abuse of any policies, processes, or directions contained within is the solitary and utter responsibility of the recipient reader. Under no circumstances will any legal responsibility or blame be held against the publisher for any reparation, damages, or monetary loss due to the information herein, either directly or indirectly.

Respective authors own all copyrights not held by the publisher.

The information herein is offered for informational purposes solely and is universal as so. The presentation of the information is without a contract or any type of guarantee assurance.

The trademarks that are used are without any consent, and the publication of the trademark is without permission or backing by the trademark owner. All trademarks and brands within this book are for clarifying purposes only and are owned by the owners themselves, not affiliated with this document.

TABLE OF CONTENTS

ORIGINS OF INDIAN CUISINE..2

CHARACTERISTICS OF INDIAN CUISINE...5

MAIN INGREDIENTS...8

LENTIL RECIPES..14

    SPICED COCONUT LENTILS..14

    HEALTHY LENTIL CURRY..16

    DELICIOUS BLACK LENTIL CURRY..18

    LENTIL BUTTERNUT SQUASH CURRY..20

    SIMPLE SLOW COOKER LENTIL..21

    LENTIL POTATO COCONUT CURRY..22

    SPICY LENTIL STEW..23

    GLUTEN FREE MASALA LENTILS..25

    FLAVORFUL RED LENTILS CURRY..26

    CAULIFLOWER LENTIL CURRY..27

    DELICIOUS TEMPERED LENTILS...28

    LENTIL SWEET POTATO SOUP...30

    POTATO RED LENTIL CURRY..32

    HEALTHY SPINACH LENTILS...34

    EASY LENTILS RICE...35

    LENTIL CHICKEN VEGETABLE CURRY...36

    HEALTHY GREEN LENTIL CURRY...37

    SMOKEY LENTIL SOUP..38

    SPINACH COCONUT LENTIL SOUP...39

- Spicy Keema Lentils ... 41
- Creamy Split Pea Curry ... 42
- Lentil Vegetable Soup ... 43
- Delicious Lemon Lentils ... 44
- Tasty Carrot Lentils Soup ... 45
- Lentil Sweet Potato Beans Stew ... 46

BEANS AND PEAS RECIPES ... 48
- Healthy Chickpeas and Tofu ... 48
- Chickpea Pumpkin Lentil Curry ... 50
- North Indian red Beans ... 51
- Simple Black Eyed Peas ... 53
- Tasty Black Eyed Pea Curry ... 54
- Healthy Green Pea and Cauliflower Korma ... 55
- Red Beans Bowl ... 56
- Chickpea Lentil Chili ... 58
- Red Beans and Lentils ... 59
- Simple Chickpea Curry ... 61
- Pea Chickpea Vegetable Curry ... 62
- Perfect Curried Baked Beans ... 63
- Red Beans with Bell Pepper ... 65
- Spicy Black Eyed Peas ... 66
- Chickpea Coconut Quinoa Curry ... 67
- Red Beans Cabbage Soup ... 68
- Gluten Free Chickpea Curry ... 69
- Vegetarian Chili Bowl ... 71
- Healthy Turmeric Lentil Bean Chili ... 73

Chickpea Kale Sweet Potato Stew...74

Chickpea Spinach Cauliflower Curry...76

Spicy Winter Chickpeas...78

Spicy Curried Chickpeas..80

Spiced Green Peas Rice...82

Buttered Peas Rice..83

VEGETABLE RECIPES..84

Delicious Spiced Potatoes and Cauliflower..84

Scrumptious Spinach Paneer...86

Tasty Spinach Potato..87

Spicy Eggplant Potatoes...88

Healthy Vegetable Coconut Curry...89

Easy Whole Cauliflower Curry..90

Vegetable Curried Rice...91

Curried Zucchini Eggplant..92

Flavourful Vegetable Korma..93

Potato Okra Curry..94

Delicious Navratan Korma...95

Slow Cooker Sambar..96

Creamy Carrot Squash Soup..97

Yummy Slow Cooked Potatoes..98

Curried Potatoes..100

Mushroom Eggplant Potato Curry...101

ggplant Chickpea Curry..103

Coconut Eggplant Curry...104

Creamy Cauliflower Soup..105

- Delicious Sweet Potato Curry 107
- Flavorful Vegetable Curry 109
- Delicious Tofu Coconut Curry 110
- Creamy Coconut Pumpkin Curry 111
- Hearty Potato Curry 112
- Mix Vegetable Curry 114

MEAT RECIPES 115
- Tasty Chicken Tikka Masala 115
- Delicious Chicken Tandoori 117
- Peanut Butter Chicken 118
- Spicy Chicken Curry 119
- Juicy and Tender Goat Curry 121
- Delicious Slow Cooked Beef 123
- Simple Beef Curry 125
- Easy Curried Chicken 127
- Chicken Vegetable Curry 128
- Spicy Cauliflower Chicken 129
- Yummy Butter Chicken 130
- Lamb Curry 132
- Chicken Quinoa Curry 134
- Delicious Chicken Stew 135
- Creamy Coconut Chicken Curry 136
- Tasty Chicken Kheema 137
- Shredded Lamb 139
- Yummy Chicken Soup 141
- Sweet Beef Curry 142

Indian Cookbook

YELLOW CHICKEN CURRY..143

SPINACH LAMB CURRY...144

CLASSIC LAMB CURRY..146

EASY LAMB STEW..149

SPICY BEEF ROAST...151

SPICY BEEF STEW..152

Origins of Indian Cuisine

Speaking univocally about Indian cuisine makes little sense: due to the extreme variety of environments, climatic areas, religious food precepts adopted by the numerous communities (Sikhs, Muslims, Buddhists, Christians, Jainists, Hindus).
Having said this, it must be said that the most widespread "schools" in the West are those typical of the cuisine of the north, a synthesis of Punjabi and Kashmire traditions, greatly influenced by Persian influences (parsi) and by the Islamic invasions suffered under the Mughal dynasty (Mughlai cuisine) .

Indian cuisine is arguably the spiciest in the world. This is the homeland of pepper, cinnamon and cardamom. From time immemorial cloves, nutmeg, mace, ginger, turmeric and cumin, grown in India and neighboring regions, have been key ingredients in all regional traditions of the area. It is hard to believe that chilli, abundant especially in the very spicy dishes of the southern area, only made its appearance in India in the 16th century.

In general, the art of the Baburchi, the Indian chef, revolves around the art of mixing and dosing spices (masala) in his dishes, not only to obtain that typical taste but also to make the most of the virtues of the "active ingredients" contained by herbs, rhizomes and spices, as taught by Ayurvedic science. There are many recipes, but almost all of them use from five to twenty different spices, and already in the Renaissance there were about 300 different aromas. It is also essential to master the marinating techniques to flavor and tenderize the meats, cooked in the tandoor, a particular vertical oven in terracotta in the shape of a wineskin.

In general, the Koranic and Hindu food precepts are valid: with the banning of pork and beef, to the advantage of chicken and lamb, the use of some special techniques, such as marinating meat in a mixture of yogurt and spices prior to grilling (seekh kebab). About eighty percent of the Indian population follows a vegetarian diet with the consumption of a lot of rice (chaaval), legumes (dhal) and exotic vegetables (bitter melon, okra, drumstick, loofah).

Throughout the Indian subcontinent there is a widespread tradition of serving the meal on a tray with many bowls (thali), made of metal in the north, replaced by a banana leaf in the south. A thali consists of many small portions: rice boiled in white (basmati or patna) or sauteed with spices, vegetables and dried fruit (pulao), stewed legumes (dal, chana, toovar, urad, masoor), and many mostly unleavened wheat breads, flavored with herbs and spices, cooked in the tandoor oven, grilled or fried (chapati, naan, paratha, roti, puris).

On the table there is never a shortage of sauces: refreshing based on yogurt or coconut milk and spices; spicy based on vegetables and tropical fruit (chatny, achar, pickles), served with crispy chickpea flour wraps (pappadam).

Do not forget the excellent desserts prepared with reduced buffalo milk and flavored in the north with saffron and cardamom, in the south with coconut milk. The offer of desserts continues with pistachio or mango pulp ice-creams (piste or mango kulfi), spoon desserts with rice and spices (kheer, firni), fried batter boulettes in rose syrup (gulabjamun), all sometimes decorated with edible leaves of gold and silver, as was the custom in the royal banquets of the Maharajahs.

Characteristics of Indian Cuisine

Indian cuisine is very varied and its characteristics are the result of various climatic, historical, religious and philosophical factors. Eating is considered an integral part of the spiritual experience. India is a country rich in natural products. In the Indus Valley, the development of agriculture and cattle breeding took place 7000 years before Christ. The climate has always made a variety of foods and spices available in different areas of the country. Invasions of foreigners and commercial contacts have introduced Arab, Chinese, Mongolian, Turkish, Muslim, English and Portuguese influences into Indian cuisine.

Muslims (with the Mughal period) introduced, for example, kebabs or specialties such as biryani and pulao (consisting of rice mixed with spiced meats or vegetables) and various types of fruit such as peaches, apricots, plums, melons, citrus fruits and so on. Despite the regional variations, the common denominators of the cuisine are the use of rice, but also of bread and legumes as basic foods, as well as the enrichment of flavors and aromas through spices and sauces. The methods of preparing the dishes are many. In addition to frying, slow cooking (stewed foods) is preferred.

The term curry, in addition to indicating a mixture of spices, also means sauce and also food (meat, fish or vegetables) cooked in a liquid base. In South India, especially Tamil, there are sambar or rasam, stews based on lentils (dal) and various vegetables including carrots, okra, pumpkin, onions or tomatoes and so on, flavored with tamarind, coriander, turmeric, chilli and other spices. In the North, cooking bases and sauces using dairy products prevail (milk, cream, yogurt or Panir cheese).

Also in the northern region is the tandoor, a particular oven lined with clay and underground, used to cook meats and breads through the heat of the walls. The word taliindicates a meal consisting of several foods, condiments and breads, served on a round steel tray, often stainless, (today also in plastic), with raised edges and divided into sectors, on which both the foods are placed, and some bowls, always metallic, for liquid foods (soups and sauces). The chaats are "out of meals", usually purchased along the streets from street vendors or in some places, served on small metal plates or in containers of banana leaves. Typical components are puffed rice, puri (stuffed fried breads), samosas (a sort of fried salty dough, with a pyramidal shape, stuffed with potatoes, onion,Panir cheese, peas or meat, mint, tamarind, cilantro or other spices), papdi (a kind of fried crackers), mashed potatoes and so on.

These preparations are often added with onion, tomato, peppers, fresh mango or pomegranate seeds, seasoned with chutney or yogurt and spiced with chaat masala which combines, for example, ginger, dried mango powder, cumin, coriander, pepper and black salt.

Main Ingredients

Cereals and legumes

In India, rice is a fundamental component of cooking. Particular varieties such as basmati or patna are also produced and used. As an accompaniment to food, in addition to rice, wheat or legume bread is consumed, often unleavened, cooked on a plate, in the oven, or even for frying. Chapati is a kind of flatbread cooked on a tava or hot circular plate, while roti has the same characteristics but is seasoned with butter and enriched with seeds. Fried breads, also very popular, include the parati, the puri and the pappadumi, made from chickpea flour. Common leavened breads are naan, baked in the oven. Cereals, especially rice and semolina, are also used in the preparation of desserts. Legumes (there are more than 50 varieties), peas, beans and lentils of various types and colors are consumed in abundance especially by vegetarians. Pre-treated varieties are also used (peeled, with cuticle removal and then crushed, more quickly cooked). Dal are preparations, of practically daily use, based on whole legumes or more often peeled and crushed (dal in Sanskrit means "broken"), eaten with rice or bread. The procedure is simple: boiled legumes, sometimes with the addition of ginger, tamarind and immature mango, are added with garlic and onion and a mixture of spices and aromas (called tadka or baghaar) composed of cumin, coriander, chilli or a mixture of spices (garam masala), dissolved in a little hot oil.

Meat and fish

In India, various religious precepts lead to the exclusion of certain types of meat from food, including, for example, cattle (for Hindus) or pork (for Muslims) or all types of meat (for Hindu vegetarians, Buddhists or Jains). The consumption of meat is often not specifically prohibited, however it is implicit in the Hindu concept of ahimsa or non-violence and respect for all life forms. Even non-vegetarian Hindus still exclude the consumption of beef. Cows are considered sacred as they provide milk and dairy products, support agricultural work, and their excreta serve as fertilizer and fuel. The slaughter of cattle is prohibited by law in some states (Kerala and Arunachal Pradesh). The consumption of milk and derivatives is however allowed and is indeed very widespread as an integral part of various culinary preparations. A vegetarian diet is now followed by about 30% of the population.

Milk and derivatives

Ghee is the traditional clarified butter of Indian cuisine. It is prepared by heating the fresh butter in order to eliminate the water (the butter contains 15%) and to deposit the proteins on the bottom of the container. These processes favor the preservation of the product, even without refrigeration, and make it more resistant to high cooking temperatures. Yogurt is also very popular, especially the compact or dahi type, obtained by filtration, in order to eliminate excess buttermilk. Yoghurt is variously used as a drink (for example lassi is composed of natural yogurt diluted with water and flavored with lemon juice and cumin), in the preparation of sauces (for example raita or pachadi composed of spiced yogurt, with coriander, cumin, mint, pepper and vegetables such as cucumbers or onion), as a basis for diluting spices and in the preparation of various dishes, especially in the north of the country. In the South, a food of practically daily use is thayirsadam, or rice and yogurt prepared by mixing yogurt with simple or spiced boiled rice, sometimes with the addition of dal. Panir, on the other hand, is a cheese produced in the northern regions of India.

Vegetables and fruit

There are numerous varieties of vegetables and fruit of different origins. Mango is widely used, consumed in a variety of ways: fresh, ripe, but also unripe and sour, with the addition of salt and sometimes of chili pepper or in the form of juice or, again, in the preparation of chutneys, or dry (in strips or blocks) or pulverized to add to spice mixtures. Coconut and its milk are used in the preparation of savory and sweet dishes, or drinks, especially in the South.

Spices and herbs

Indian cuisine involves an intense use of spices, added to virtually all types of foods, from meat to fish, legumes and cereals, vegetables, drinks and sweets. The most common are cardamom, cloves, coriander, cumin, nutmeg, fenugreek, pepper, paprika, chilli, mustard, tamarind, turmeric, saffron and ginger. Some spices, including nutmeg, mace and cloves, were imported from Indonesia, while coriander and cumin were introduced from the Mediterranean area by Arab traders. Curry or garam masala are blends of spices.

The latter is made up of at least five types among which cardamom, cinnamon and cloves prevail, in curries instead there are mainly cumin, cardamom, coriander and turmeric, but also other varieties. The type of spice, the total quantity and the proportions between the different components contribute to the aroma and the degree of spiciness achieved in the various preparations. Spices to be mixed with foods are mostly diluted in a liquid base, for example yogurt, dahi, or coconut milk or in small quantities of heated oil.

Seasonings

As already described, butter (ghee) is a very popular condiment, but various types of plant products are also used, including mustard seed oil, with a pungent flavor, high in erucic acid, considered harmful in other countries, soy or sunflower oils, coconut butter and vegetable margarines. A very special condiment is black salt, an unrefined coarse salt extracted from Indian mines, containing not only sodium chloride but also iron and sulfur salts that give foods a particular flavor. Chutneys are sauces with a more or less sweet and pungent flavor, originating from Southeast Asia and widely used, composed of vegetables or fruits including, for example, tomato, onion, garlic or mango (using unripe fruits and therefore with a sour taste), lime, peaches, dates, tamarind and so on, herbs and spices including chili peppers that make these products spicy.

Drinks

The most consumed drink is tea, often taken with spiced and sweetened milk; however, coffee also has a certain diffusion, especially in the south of the continent. Other refreshing drinks are based on dairy products (lassi made with yogurt or badamdood, milk spiced with cardamom), coconut or other fruit.

LENTIL RECIPES

Spiced Coconut Lentils
Total Time: 8 hours 20 minutes
Serves: 12

Ingredients

3 cups yellow lentils, Soak for 10 minutes
14 oz coconut milk
1/4 cup cilantro
1 tbsp fresh ginger, peeled and chopped
2 tbsp curry powder
2 tsp ground cumin
2 tsp ground turmeric
1 tsp chili powder
4 chilies, stemmed and seeded
1 large onion, chopped
5 garlic cloves
1/2 tsp sugar
28 oz can tomatoes, diced
Kosher salt

Directions

Rinse lentil and drain well. Add lentil into the slow cooker.

Add sugar, chili powder, turmeric, cumin, curry powder, ginger, garlic, onion, and Serrano chilies into the food processor and process until mixture becomes a paste. Add into the slow cooker.

Stir in tomatoes and 6 cups of water.

Cover slow cooker and cook on low for 8 hours.

Season with salt and stir well.

Add coconut milk and stir well.

Garnish with cilantro and serve.

Calories 258, Fat 8 g, Carbohydrates 33 g, Sugar 4 g, Protein 13 g, Cholesterol 0 mg

Healthy Lentil Curry

Total Time: 5 hours 10 minutes
Serves: 6

Ingredients

1 1/2 cups green lentils, rinse and drained
3 tbsp tomato paste
14 oz can coconut milk
3 tsp curry powder
1 onion, diced
3 garlic cloves, minced
1 yellow pepper, diced
1/4 tsp pepper
1/2 tsp ground ginger
2 tsp garam masala
2 tsp sugar
2 1/2 cups water
2 tbsp olive oil
1 tsp garlic powder
1 tsp cumin
1 1/2 tsp salt

Directions

Add olive oil, yellow pepper, garlic, and onion into the slow cooker.
Add lentils into the slow cooker and stir well.
Add all remaining ingredients and stir well.

Chef Marino

Cover and cook on low for 5 hours.
Stir well and serve with rice.

Calories 376, Fat 19 g, Carbohydrates 39 g, Sugar 4 g, Protein 15 g, Cholesterol 0 mg

Delicious Black Lentil Curry

Total Time: 12 hours 15 minutes

Serves: 8

Ingredients

1 cup whole black gram lentils
3 cloves
1 tbsp ginger, chopped
8 garlic cloves, chopped
2 green chilies, cut lengthwise
1 tbsp coriander powder
1/2 tsp turmeric powder
1/2 cup kidney beans
1 bay leaf
1 cinnamon stick
3 cardamom pods
1/2 tsp chili powder
4 tomatoes, diced
1 tsp garam masala
1/4 cup cream
2 tbsp butter
Salt

Directions

Soak black lentils and kidney beans in water for overnight.

Chef Marino

Add all ingredients except cream into the slow cooker with 4
cups water and stir well.
Cover and cook on low for 12 hours.
Stir well and lightly mash using the back of a spoon.
Add cream and stir well.
Serve and enjoy.

Calories 186, Fat 4 g, Carbohydrates 27 g, Sugar 2 g, Protein 10 g, Cholesterol 9 mg

Lentil Butternut Squash Curry

Total Time: 12 hours 15 minutes
Serves: 8

Ingredients

2 cups red lentils
4 cups butternut squash, cut into cubes
2 tbsp ginger, minced
1 1/2 tsp curry powder
1 tsp ground coriander
1 onion, minced
2 garlic cloves, minced
1 tsp garam masala
1 tsp turmeric
14 oz can coconut milk
19 oz can tomatoes, diced
3 cups vegetable stock
1 tsp ground cumin
1/2 tsp salt

Directions

Add all ingredients into the slow cooker and stir well.
Cover and cook on low for 8 hours.
Serve and enjoy.

Calories 329, Fat 11 g, Carbohydrates 45 g, Sugar 5 g, Protein 15 g, Cholesterol 0 mg

Chef Marino

Simple Slow Cooker Lentil

Total Time: 6 hours 15 minutes
Serves: 6

Ingredients

2 cups red lentils, rinsed and drained
1 bay leaf
1 tbsp ground turmeric
1 tbsp fresh ginger, grated
1 medium onion, diced
15 oz can tomatoes, diced
5 cups water
1 tsp fennel seeds
2 tsp mustard seeds
2 tsp cumin seeds
1/4 tsp ground black pepper
1 tsp kosher salt

Directions

Heat pan over medium heat and toast fennel seeds, mustard seeds, and cumin seeds in a pan until fragrant for 2-3 minutes. Add toasted spices and remaining all ingredients into the slow cooker and stir well.
Cover and cook on low for 6 hours.
Stir well and serve.

Calories 265, Fat 1 g, Carbohydrates 46 g, Sugar 4 g, Protein 18 g, Cholesterol 0 mg

Indian Cookbook

Lentil Potato Coconut Curry

Total Time: 8 hours 15 minutes

Serves: 10

Ingredients

2 cups brown lentils
14 oz can coconut milk
3 cups vegetable broth
15 oz can tomato sauce
15 oz can tomatoes, diced
1/4 tsp ground cloves
3 tbsp curry powder
2 medium carrots, peel and diced
1 sweet potato, peel and diced
2 garlic cloves, minced
1 medium onion, diced

Directions

Add all ingredients except coconut milk into the slow cooker
and stir well.

Cover and cook on low for 8 hours.

Stir in coconut milk and serve with rice.

Calories 152, Fat 3 g, Carbohydrates 22 g, Sugar 6 g, Protein 9 g, Cholesterol 0 mg

Chef Marino

Spicy Lentil Stew

Total Time: 6 hours 15 minutes
Serves: 8

Ingredients

3 cups red lentils, rinsed and drained
3 1/2 cup tomatoes, crushed
1/2 tbsp black pepper
1/2 tbsp curry powder
1/2 tbsp paprika
1/2 tbsp chili powder
1/2 tbsp garam masala
1/2 tbsp turmeric powder
6 cups vegetable broth
1 onion, diced
2 garlic cloves, minced
3 Serrano chili, diced
2 tbsp cilantro, minced
1 tbsp Creole seasoning
1 tbsp garlic powder
1 tbsp onion powder
1/2 tbsp ginger powder

Directions

Add all ingredients into the slow cooker and stir well.

Cover and cook on high for 5 hours.

Uncover the slow cooker and cook for another 50 minutes.

Serve and enjoy.

Calories 318, Fat 2 g, Carbohydrates 51 g, Sugar 5 g, Protein 23 g, Cholesterol 0 mg

Chef Marino

Gluten Free Masala Lentils

Total Time: 6 hours 10 minutes
Serves: 8

Ingredients

2 1/4 cups brown lentils
4 cups vegetable broth
15 oz can tomatoes, diced
1 medium onion, chopped
3 garlic cloves, minced
1 tbsp fresh ginger, minced
1/4 cup tomato paste
2 tsp tamarind paste
1 tsp maple syrup
1 1/2 tsp garam masala
1 cup coconut milk
3/4 tsp salt

Directions

Add all ingredients except coconut milk into the slow cooker
and stir well.
Cover and cook on low for 6 hours.

Stir in coconut milk and serve.

Calories 306, Fat 9 g, Carbohydrates 41 g, Sugar 5 g, Protein 17 g, Cholesterol 0 mg

Flavorful Red Lentils Curry

Total Time: 8 hours 15 minutes

Serves: 16

Ingredients

4 cups brown lentils, rinsed and drained
5 tbsp red curry paste
1 tbsp garam masala
1 1/2 tsp turmeric
2 tsp sugar
1/2 cup coconut milk
29 oz can tomato puree
2 onions, diced
4 garlic cloves, minced
1 tbsp ginger, minced
4 tbsp butter
7 cups water
1 tsp salt

Directions

Add all ingredients except coconut milk into the slow cooker and stir well.
Cover and cook on low for 8 hours.
Add coconut milk and stir well.
Serve with rice and enjoy.

Calories 261, Fat 6 g, Carbohydrates 37 g, Sugar 4 g, Protein 13 g, Cholesterol 8 mg

Chef Marino

Cauliflower Lentil Curry

Total Time: 5 hours 15 minutes
Serves: 6

Ingredients

1 cup red lentils
3 cups cauliflower, cut into florets
3 dates, pitted and chopped
2/3 cup coconut milk
1 1/2 tsp turmeric
1 tsp ginger, grated
2 tbsp Thai red curry paste
3 garlic cloves, minced
1/2 onion, chopped
3 cups vegetable broth
1/4 tsp sea salt

Directions

Add all ingredients except coconut milk into the slow cooker and stir well.

Cover and cook on low for 5 hours.

Add coconut milk and stir well.
Serve with rice and enjoy.

Calories 247, Fat 9 g, Carbohydrates 29 g, Sugar 6 g, Protein 12 g, Cholesterol 0 mg

Delicious Tempered Lentils

Total Time: 6 hours 20 minutes
Serves: 6

Ingredients

1 1/2 cups yellow split lentils, rinsed and drained
1/4 cup fresh cilantro, chopped
1 tsp turmeric powder
2 tsp garlic, minced
2 medium tomatoes, chopped
1/2 medium onion, chopped
1 tsp salt
For tempering:
2 tbsp vegetable oil
1/4 tsp chili powder
1/2 tsp coriander powder
1/2 tsp cumin powder
1 garlic cloves, minced
1/2 tsp whole cumin seeds

Directions

Add lentils into the slow cooker with 4 cups water.

Add turmeric powder, garlic, tomatoes, onion, and salt into the slow cooker and stir well.

Cover and cook on low for 5 hours.

Heat vegetable oil in the pan over medium-high heat.

Once the oil is hot then turn off the heat and add cumin, garlic, and spices. Mix well.

Stir prepared tempering into the hot lentil.

Add cilantro and stir well.

Cook lentils for another 1 hour to blend all flavors.

Serve hot with rice and enjoy.

Calories 208, Fat 5.2 g, Carbohydrates 28 g, Sugar 1.5 g, Protein 12.7 g, Cholesterol 0 mg

Lentil Sweet Potato Soup

Total Time: 6 hours 20 minutes
Serves: 4

Ingredients

1 1/2 cups brown lentils
1 large sweet potato, cut into 1/2 inch cubes
6 cups vegetable broth
1 cup coconut milk
1/2 tbsp chili paste
1 medium onion, diced
3 garlic cloves, minced
1/2 tbsp ginger, grated
2 tsp ground cumin
1 tsp garam masala
2 tsp lime juice
1/4 cup fresh cilantro, chopped
14 oz can tomatoes, diced
Pepper
Salt

Directions

Add all ingredients except tomatoes and lime juice into the slow cooker and stir well.

Cover and cook on low for 6 hours.

Chef Marino

Stir in tomatoes and lime juice.

Cook soup for another 10 minutes to blend the flavors.

Season with pepper and salt.

Serve warm and enjoy.

Calories 395, Fat 17 g, Carbohydrates 54 g, Sugar 11 g, Protein 23 g, Cholesterol 1 mg

Potato Red Lentil Curry

Total Time: 4 hours 15 minutes
Serves: 8

Ingredients

1 cup red lentils, rinsed
2 potatoes, cut into cubed
1 cup brown lentil, rinsed
1 large onion, diced
1/2 tsp turmeric
1/2 tsp cumin seeds, toasted
1 tsp sugar
14 oz can tomato, diced
14 oz can coconut milk
1 tbsp garlic, minced
1 tsp ginger, minced
2 tbsp butter
2 tbsp curry powder
1/2 tsp red pepper flakes

Directions

Add all ingredients except coconut milk into the slow cooker
and stir well.

Add water into the slow cooker to cover lentil mixture.

Chef Marino

Cover and cook on high for 4 hours.

Add coconut milk and stir well.

Serve warm and enjoy.

Calories 307, Fat 14 g, Carbohydrates 39 g, Sugar 3 g, Protein 13 g, Cholesterol 8 mg

Healthy Spinach Lentils

Total Time: 4 hours 30 minutes

Serves: 4

Ingredients

1 cup yellow split peas
3 1/2 cups water
10 oz spinach, chopped
1 tsp cumin seeds
1 tbsp fresh ginger, peeled and minced
3 garlic cloves, minced
1 tsp mustard seeds
1 medium onion, diced
15 oz can tomatoes, drained and diced
2 jalapeno pepper, cored and diced
1 tsp turmeric
1/2 tsp coriander
1/4 tsp cayenne
1 tsp salt

Directions

Add all ingredients except spinach into the slow cooker and stir well. Cover and cook on high for 4 hours. Add spinach and cook for another 20.
Stir well and serve.

Calories 236, Fat 1.4 g, Carbohydrates 43 g, Sugar 9 g, Protein 16.1 g, Cholesterol 0 mg

Chef Marino

Easy Lentils Rice

Total Time: 4 hours 10 minutes
Serves: 6

Ingredients

1/2 cup lentils, rinsed and drained
1 tsp garlic powder
3 1/2 cups vegetable broth
1 tbsp curry powder
1 cup white rice, rinsed and drained
1 onion, diced
1/4 tsp pepper
Salt

Directions

Add all ingredients into the slow cooker and stir well.

Cover and cook on high for 4 hours.

Stir well and serve.

Calories 204, Fat 1.3 g, Carbohydrates 37 g, Sugar 1.7 g, Protein 9.6 g, Cholesterol 0 mg

Lentil Chicken Vegetable Curry

Total Time: 4 hours 20 minutes
Serves: 8

Ingredients

1 lb dried lentils, rinsed and drained
4 cups fresh spinach, chopped
4 cups vegetable broth
1/4 tsp cinnamon
1 1/2 tsp turmeric
1/2 tsp cayenne
1 tbsp curry powder
2 lbs chicken thighs, boneless and cut into pieces
6 garlic cloves, minced
1 small cauliflower head, cut into florets
2 cups carrots, chopped
1 large onion, chopped
1 tsp salt

Directions

Add all ingredients except spinach into the slow cooker and stir well. Cover and cook on high for 3 1/2 hours. Add spinach and stir well. Cover and cook for another 30 minutes.
Stir well and serve with rice.

Calories 473, Fat 10 g, Carbohydrates 42 g, Sugar 4.6 g, Protein 51 g, Cholesterol 101 mg

Chef Marino

Healthy Green Lentil Curry

Total Time: 6 hours 15 minutes

Serves: 6

Ingredients

2 cups green lentils, rinsed and drained
3 cups water
6 oz can tomato paste
14 oz can coconut milk
1 tsp cumin
1 tsp curry powder
1/2 tsp ground coriander
1 tsp turmeric
1 tsp vegetable oil
6 garlic cloves, minced
1 large onion, chopped
1 1/4 tsp salt

Directions

Heat oil in the pan over medium heat. Add garlic and onion to the pan and sauté for 5 minutes. Add cumin, curry powder, coriander, turmeric, and salt and sauté for 1 minute. Transfer pan mixture to the slow cooker with remaining all ingredients. Stir well. Cover and cook on low for 6 hours. Serve warm with rice and enjoy.

Calories 404, Fat 15.9 g, Carbohydrates 49 g, Sugar 5.9 g, Protein 19.7 g, Cholesterol 0 mg

Smokey Lentil Soup

Total Time: 6 hours 15 minutes

Serves: 6

Ingredients

2 cups red lentils
2 tbsp smoked paprika
2 carrots, chopped
4 garlic cloves, minced
8 cups vegetable broth
1 onion, chopped
3 tbsp fresh parsley, chopped
1/4 cup hulled pumpkin seeds
2 potatoes, peeled and chopped
1/3 cup tomato paste
3 tbsp lemon juice
3 tbsp vegetable oil

Directions

Add lentils, lemon juice, tomato paste, garlic, paprika, carrots, potato, onion, and broth into the slow cooker and stir well. Cover and cook on low for 6 hours. Meanwhile, in a small bowl, combine together parsley and oil. Ladle soup into the bowls and drizzle with parsley and oil mixture. Sprinkle pumpkin seeds over the soup. Serve and enjoy.

Calories 474, Fat 9.9 g, Carbohydrates 67.6 g, Sugar 7 g, Protein 25.8 g, Cholesterol 0 mg

Chef Marino

Spinach Coconut Lentil Soup

Total Time: 4 hours 45 minutes

Serves: 6

Ingredients

4 cups fresh spinach, chopped
14 oz coconut milk
4 cups vegetable stock
1 1/2 cup red lentils, rinsed and drained
1 tsp ground cinnamon
1/2 tsp garam masala
1 tsp ground turmeric
1 tsp ground coriander seed
1 tsp ground cumin
2 tsp garlic, minced
1 large onion, chopped
1 tbsp vegetable oil
Pepper
Salt

Directions

Heat oil in the pan over medium heat.

Add onion to the pan and sauté for 5 minutes or until golden brown.

Add cinnamon, garam masala, turmeric, coriander, cumin, and garlic and cook for 2 minutes.

Transfer onion-spice mixture into the slow cooker.

Add lentils and stock into the slow cooker and stir well.

Cover and cook on low for 4 hours.

Add coconut milk and spinach. Stir well and cook for another 30 minutes.

Season with pepper and salt.

Serve and enjoy.

Calories 368, Fat 20 g, Carbohydrates 37 g, Sugar 5 g, Protein 14.9 g, Cholesterol 0 mg

Chef Marino

Spicy Keema Lentils

Total Time: 4 hours 15 minutes
Serves: 4

Ingredients

3 cups green lentils, cooked
1 tsp dried chili flakes
1/2 tsp ground turmeric
2 tsp garam masala
2 tsp ground coriander
2 tsp ground cumin
1 large onion, chopped
3 tbsp fresh ginger, grated
6 garlic cloves, chopped
1 1/2 cup vegetable broth
2 tbsp tamari
1 tsp pepper
1 tsp salt

Directions

Add all ingredients into the slow cooker and stir well.

Cover and cook on low for 4 hours.

Stir well and serve.

Calories 206, Fat 0.9 g, Carbohydrates 37 g, Sugar 2 g Protein 15 g, Cholesterol 0 mg

Creamy Split Pea Curry

Total Time: 6 hours 15 minutes
Serves: 6

Ingredients

1 1/2 cups dried split peas
1 cup heavy cream
1/2 tsp ground ginger
2 tsp curry powder
1 tbsp turmeric
1 tbsp green curry paste
3 garlic cloves, minced
1/2 cup onion, diced
15 oz can coconut milk
28 oz can tomatoes, crushed
1 tsp salt

Directions

Add all ingredients except cream into the slow cooker.
Stir well.
Cover and cook on low for 6 hours.
Add cream and stir well.
Serve with rice and enjoy.

Calories 425, Fat 23.8 g, Carbohydrates 42.4 g, Sugar 9 g, Protein 15.5 g, Cholesterol 27 mg

Chef Marino

Lentil Vegetable Soup

Total Time: 8 hours 15 minutes

Serves: 8

Ingredients

1 1/2 cups green lentils, rinsed and drained

9 cups vegetable broth

5 peppercorns

3 bay leaves

3 tbsp soy sauce

1 tsp thyme

2 tsp oregano

1 tbsp garlic powder

2 cups corn

4 cups potatoes, diced

3 large carrots, diced

3 large celery stalks, diced

2 medium onion, diced

Directions

Add all ingredients into the slow cooker and mix well. Cover and cook on low for 8 hours. Discard peppercorns and bay leaves from soup and using blender puree the soup until you get desired texture. Serve hot and enjoy.

Calories 288, Fat 2.6 g, Carbohydrates 49 g, Sugar 6.7 g, Protein 18.5 g, Cholesterol 0 mg

Delicious Lemon Lentils

Total Time: 2 hours 45 minutes

Serves: 8

Ingredients

1 1/2 cups pink lentils
1 tbsp milk
2 tbsp lemon juice
2 Serrano chilies, sliced
1 tbsp fresh ginger, minced
4 garlic cloves, sliced
1 small onion, diced
5 cups water
1 1/2 tsp salt

Directions

Add all ingredients except milk and lemon juice into the slow cooker. Stir well.

Cover and cook on high for 2 1/2 hours.

Add lemon juice and stir well.

Add milk and stir well and serve.

Calories 135, Fat 0.9 g, Carbohydrates 23.4 g, Sugar 0.6 g, Protein 9.4 g, Cholesterol 0 mg

Chef Marino

Tasty Carrot Lentils Soup

Total Time: 8 hours 15 minutes

Serves: 8

Ingredients

1/2 cup lentils
2 lbs carrots, peeled and cut into 1-inch pieces
1/2 tsp harissa
1/4 cup maple syrup
1 cup orange juice
4 cups vegetable broth
1 tsp fresh ginger, grated
1/2 tbsp ground cumin
1/2 tbsp curry powder
1 medium onion, peeled and chopped
Pepper
Salt

Directions

Add orange juice, broth, ginger, curry powder, onion, and carrots into the slow cooker and mix well.
Cover and cook on low for 6 hours.
Add lentils, harissa, and maple syrup. Stir well and cook on high for another 2 hours.
Season with pepper and salt.
Serve and enjoy.

Calories 158, Fat 1.1 g, Carbohydrates 30.6 g Sugar 15.3 g
Protein 7 g, Cholesterol 0 mg

Lentil Sweet Potato Beans Stew

Total Time: 6 hours 30 minutes

Serves: 6

Ingredients

3/4 cup dry lentils, rinsed and drained
3 cups sweet potatoes, cut into 1 inch cubed
1 1/2 cups green beans, cut into pieces
1 1/2 cups baby carrots
1/2 cup plain yogurt
1 3/4 cup vegetable broth
2 garlic cloves, minced
1 tsp fresh ginger, chopped
1 tsp ground cumin
1 tbsp curry powder
2 tbsp vegetable oil
1/4 cup onion, chopped
1/4 tsp black pepper
1/2 tsp salt

Directions

Add lentils, carrots, onion, and sweet potatoes into the slow cooker.

In a pan, heat oil over medium heat.

Add garlic, ginger, pepper, cumin, curry powder, and salt and stir for 1 minute. Stir in broth.

Pour mixture into the slow cooker and mix well.

Cover and cook on low for 6 hours.

Turn heat to high and stir in green beans. Cover and cook for another 15 minutes.

Top with plain yogurt and serve.

Calories 269, Fat 5.9 g, Carbohydrates 43.5 g, Sugar 4.8 g, Protein 10.8 g, Cholesterol 1 mg

BEANS AND PEAS RECIPES

Healthy Chickpeas and Tofu

Total Time: 4 hours 15 minutes
Serves: 6

Ingredients

12 oz firm tofu
15 oz can chickpeas, rinsed and drained
1/8 cup cilantro, chopped
1/2 tsp ground ginger
2 tsp chili powder
1 tbsp curry powder
1 tbsp garam masala
1 cup tomato puree
14 oz can coconut milk
4 garlic cloves, minced
1 medium onion, diced
1 tsp vegetable oil
Pepper
Salt

Directions

Rinse tofu well and pat dry with paper towel. Squeeze out all liquid from tofu and cut tofu into the pieces.

Heat oil in the saucepan over medium heat.

Add onion to the pan and sauté for 5 minutes.

Add garlic and cook for 1 minute.

Whisk in coconut milk, ginger, chili powder, curry powder, garam masala, tomato puree, pepper, and salt. Cook for 5 minutes.

Add chickpeas and tofu into the slow cooker.

Pour pan mixture into the slow cooker.

Cover and cook on low for 4 hours.

Garnish with cilantro and serve.

Calories 294, Fat 18.5 g, Carbohydrates 26.2 g, Sugar 3.3 g, Protein 10.8 g, Cholesterol 0 mg

Chickpea Pumpkin Lentil Curry

Total Time: 8 hours 40 minutes

Serves: 6

Ingredients

15 oz can chickpeas, rinsed and drained
1 cup pumpkin puree
1 cup lentils, rinsed and drained
15 oz can coconut milk
1/4 tsp ground cayenne pepper
1 tbsp curry powder
2 cups vegetable broth
2 garlic cloves, minced
1 medium onion, diced
1 tsp kosher salt

Directions

Add all ingredients except coconut milk into the slow cooker and stir well.

Cover and cook on low for 8 hours.

Add coconut milk and stir well. Cook for another 30 minutes.

Serve with rice and enjoy.

Calories 376, Fat 17 g, Carbohydrates 43.5 g, Sugar 3.1 g, Protein 15.7 g, Cholesterol 0 mg

North Indian red Beans

Total Time: 4 hours 15 minutes
Serves: 4

Ingredients

2 cups dry red beans, soak for overnight
2 tbsp cilantro, chopped
1 cup tomato sauce
1 cinnamon stick
1/4 tsp turmeric
1/4 tsp cayenne pepper
1/4 tsp ground coriander
1 tbsp lemon juice
4 garlic cloves, minced
1 tsp ginger, minced
1 medium onion, chopped
1 tsp cumin seeds
1 bay leaf
1 tbsp vegetable oil
1 1/2 tsp salt

Directions

Heat oil in the pan over medium heat.

Add onion, bay leaf, and cumin seeds into the pan and cook for 5 minutes.

Add dry spices and lemon juice and stir for 2 minutes.

Add beans, cinnamon stick, tomato sauce, and salt into the slow cooker.

Transfer pan mixture into the slow cooker and stir well.

Cover and cook on high for 4 hours.

Using spoon lightly mash the red beans it helps to thicken the gravy.

Garnish with cilantro and serve.

Calories 376, Fat 4.8 g, Carbohydrates 64.1 g, Sugar 5.9 g, Protein 22.2 g, Cholesterol 0 mg

Chef Marino

Simple Black Eyed Peas

Total Time: 6 hours 15 minutes

Serves: 6

Ingredients

1 lb dried black-eyed peas, soak for overnight

1 tsp ground sage

1/8 tsp thyme

1 bay leaf

1 garlic clove, diced

1 small onion, diced

2 cups water

2 cups vegetable broth

1/2 tsp pepper

1 tsp sea salt

Directions

Add all ingredients into the slow cooker and mix well.

Cover and cook on low for 6 hours.

Serve and enjoy.

Calories 203, nFat 0.5 g, Carbohydrates 48.8 g, Sugar 2.8 g, Protein 20.2 g, Cholesterol 0 mg

Indian Cookbook

Tasty Black Eyed Pea Curry

Total Time: 4 hours 15 minutes

Serves: 4

Ingredients

1 cup dried black-eyed peas, soaked for overnight
1 bay leaf
6 garlic cloves, minced
1/2 tsp black pepper
1/4 tsp cayenne
2 tomatoes, chopped
3 cups water
1 tsp ginger, minced
1 tsp turmeric
1/2 tsp cumin seeds
1 large onion, diced
1 tsp garam masala
1 tsp salt

Directions

Add all ingredients into the slow cooker and stir well.

Cover and cook on high for 4 hours.

Stir well and serve.

Calories 128, Fat 0.4 g, Carbohydrates 31.4 g, Sugar 4.3 g, Protein 10.4 gCholesterol 0 mg

Chef Marino

Healthy Green Pea and Cauliflower Korma

Total Time: 4 hours 15 minutes

Serves: 4

Ingredients

10 oz green peas
1 cauliflower head, cut into florets
1 cup water
1 1/2 cups coconut milk
1/4 tsp cayenne
1 tsp turmeric
1/4 tsp cumin
2 tsp garam masala
1 medium onion, diced

Directions

Add all ingredients into the slow cooker and stir well.

Cover and cook on low for 4 hours.

Stir well and serve.

Calories 295, Fat 21.9 g, Carbohydrates 21.8 g, Sugar 9.8 g, Protein 7.6 g, Cholesterol 0 mg

Red Beans Bowl

Total Time: 8 hours 15 minutes
Serves: 4

Ingredients

14 oz can kidney beans, drained and rinsed
1/2 tsp garam Masala
1/2 tsp turmeric powder
2 cups onion, chopped
1 tomato, chopped
1/2 inch cinnamon stick
1 bay leaf
2 cloves
1 tsp ginger, minced
5 garlic cloves, minced
1 green chili, chopped
1/2 tbsp cumin seeds
1 tsp cayenne pepper
1 tbsp paprika
Salt

Directions

Add all ingredients except yogurt into the slow cooker and stir well.

Add 4 cups water and stir to combine.

Cover and cook on high for 8 hours.

Using back of spoon mash few beans.

Stir well and serve with rice.

Calories 399, Fat 2.1 g, Carbohydrates 72.2 g, Sugar 7.4 g, Protein 25.6 g, Cholesterol 2 mg

Chickpea Lentil Chili

Total Time: 8 hours 15 minutes

Serves: 6

Ingredients

1 cup dried chickpeas, soaked overnight
1/2 cup raisins
2 1/2 cups vegetable broth
1/2 cup water
28 oz can whole tomatoes, undrained and crushed
2 cups sweet potatoes, cut into cubes
1 cup lentils
1/2 tsp chili powder
1/2 tsp ground cinnamon
1/4 tsp ground turmeric
1 cup onion, chopped
5 garlic cloves, minced
1 1/2 tsp ground cumin
1 tsp kosher salt

Directions

Add all ingredients into the slow cooker and stir well.
Cover and cook on low for 8 hours.
Stir well and serve.

Calories 388, Fat 3.3 g, Carbohydrates 73.3 g, Sugar 17.3 g, Protein 19.6 g, Cholesterol 0 mg

Chef Marino

Red Beans and Lentils

Total Time: 4 hours 15 minutes

Serves: 10

Ingredients

3 cups red beans, cooked
1 cup black lentils, rinsed and drained
1/4 tsp ground mustard
1/4 tsp ground nutmeg
1 tsp ground turmeric
1 tsp ground cardamom
1 1/2 tsp chili powder
3 tsp ground cumin
2 tbsp ginger, grated
6 garlic cloves, minced
5 cups water
For serving:
1 tsp garam masala
2 tsp ginger, grated
2 tsp tomato paste
1/2 cup cashew creamer
Salt

Directions

Add all ingredients except serving ingredients into the slow
cooker and stir well.

Cover and cook on high for 4 hours.

Add all serving ingredients and stir well.

Serve with rice and enjoy.

Calories 288, Fat 2.8 g, Carbohydrates 49.1 g, Sugar 2 g, Protein 18.4 g, Cholesterol 0 mg

Chef Marino

Simple Chickpea Curry

Total Time: 6 hours 10 minutes
Serves: 6

Ingredients

15 oz can chickpeas
15 oz can coconut milk
15 oz can tomatoes, diced
1/4 tbsp cilantro, chopped
2 tbsp curry powder
1 tsp ginger, minced
4 garlic cloves, minced
2 onions, diced
Salt

Directions

Add all ingredients except cilantro into the slow cooker and stir well.

Cover and cook on low for 6 hours.

Garnish with cilantro and serve.

Calories 265, Fat 16.3 g, Carbohydrates 27.1 g, Sugar 4.1 g, Protein 6.4 g, Cholesterol 0 mg

Pea Chickpea Vegetable Curry

Total Time: 2 hours 15 minutes

Serves: 8

Ingredients

1 cup can chickpeas, drained
1 cup green peas
1 tsp red pepper flakes
1 tsp ground coriander
1 tsp ginger powder
2 tbsp curry powder
15 oz can coconut milk
2 cups vegetable broth
1 medium onion, diced
3/4 cup carrot, diced
1 1/2 cups potatoes, chopped
2 tsp sea salt

Directions

Add all ingredients into the slow cooker and stir well.

Cover and cook on high for 2 hours.

Stir well and serve.

Calories 201, Fat 12.4 g, Carbohydrates 19 g, Sugar 2.7 g, Protein 5.7 g, Cholesterol 0 mg

Chef Marino

Perfect Curried Baked Beans

Total Time: 8 hours 10 minutes
Serves: 8

Ingredients

4 cups pinto beans, cooked
1 tbsp vegetable oil
1 medium onion, diced
14 oz can coconut milk
6 oz can tomato paste
2 tbsp brown sugar
1 garlic cloves, minced
1 tbsp fresh ginger, minced
3 tsp curry powder
1/8 tsp red pepper flakes
1/2 tsp cumin
1/2 tsp salt

Directions

Add cooked beans into the slow cooker.
Heat oil in the pan over medium heat.
Add onion and sauté for 5 minutes.
Add garlic and sauté for another 1 minute.
Stir in crushed red peppers, cumin, curry powder, ginger, and salt.
Reduce heat and stir in coconut milk, brown sugar, and tomato paste.

Pour pan mixture over the beans and stir well.
Cover slow cooker and cook on low for 8 hours.
Serve and enjoy.

Calories 485, Fat 13 g, Carbohydrates 70.4 g, Sugar 7.4 g, Protein 22.9 g, Cholesterol 0 mg

Chef Marino

Red Beans with Bell Pepper

Total Time: 5 hours 10 minutes

Serves: 4

Ingredients

3/4 cup celery, chopped
1 tsp dried thyme
1 tsp paprika
3/4 tsp ground red pepper
1/2 tsp ground black pepper
3 cups water
1 cup dried red beans
1 cup onion, chopped
1 cup green bell pepper, chopped
14 oz turkey sausage, sliced
1 bay leaf
5 garlic cloves, minced
1/2 tsp salt

Directions

Add all ingredients into the slow cooker and stir well.

Cover and cook on high for 5 hours.

Stir well and serve with rice.

Calories 525, Fat 29 g, Carbohydrates 35.8 g, Sugar 4.1 g, Protein 30.8 g, Cholesterol 83 mg

Spicy Black Eyed Peas

Total Time: 6 hours 30 minutes

Serves: 10

Ingredients

1 lb dried black-eyed peas, rinsed and drained
1 tsp ground black pepper
1 1/2 tsp cumin
1/2 tsp cayenne pepper
1 jalapeno pepper, seeded and minced
1 red bell pepper, seeded and diced
2 garlic cloves, diced
1 onion, diced
6 cups water
Salt

Directions

Add all ingredients into the slow cooker and stir well.

Cover and cook on low for 6 hours.

Serve and enjoy.

Calories 122, Fat 0.2 g, Carbohydrates 30.7 g, Sugar 2.4 g, Protein 11.4 g, Cholesterol 0 mg

Chef Marino

Chickpea Coconut Quinoa Curry

Total Time: 4 hours 20 minutes

Serves: 8

Ingredients

3 cups sweet potato, peeled and cut into cubes
2 cups broccoli florets
14.5 oz can coconut milk
1/4 cup quinoa
2 garlic cloves, minced
1 tbsp ginger, grated
1 cup onion, diced
15 oz can chickpeas, drained and rinsed
28 oz can tomatoes, diced
1 tsp ground turmeric
2 tsp tamari
1 tsp chili flakes

Directions

Add all ingredients into the slow cooker and stir well.

Cover and cook on high for 4 hours.

Serve and enjoy.

Calories 291, Fat 12.2 g, Carbohydrates 41.3 g, Sugar 9.3 g, Protein 7.9 g, Cholesterol 0 mg

Red Beans Cabbage Soup

Total Time: 8 hours 10 minutes

Serves: 6

Ingredients

15 oz can red beans, drained and rinsed

4 cups water

4 garlic cloves, minced

1 bay leaf

1 tsp dried thyme

5 oz can tomato paste

1/2 head green cabbage, chopped

1 green bell pepper, seeded and diced

1 medium onion, diced

1 medium carrots, peeled and diced

1/4 tsp black pepper

Salt

Directions

Add all ingredients into the slow cooker and stir well.

Cover and cook on high for 8 hours.

Stir well and serve.

Calories 275, Fat 0.9 g, Carbohydrates 51.9 g, Sugar 8.6 g, Protein 18.4 g, Cholesterol 0 mg

Chef Marino

Gluten Free Chickpea Curry

Total Time: 4 hours 10 minutes
Serves: 4

Ingredients

14 oz can chickpeas, drained
3 cup sweet potatoes, peeled and chopped
1/2 tsp chili flakes
1 tbsp honey
1 tsp ground cumin
2 tsp ground turmeric
2 tsp garam masala
13 oz can cream
1 tsp vegetable oil
1 tbsp fresh ginger, grated
4 garlic cloves, minced
1 large onion, chopped

Directions

Heat oil in the pan over medium heat.

Add onion, garlic, and ginger to the pan and sauté for 5 minutes.

Add onion mixture into the blender along with honey, spices, cream, and salt and blend until smooth.

Add remaining ingredients and curry blend into the slow cooker
and stir well.

Cover and cook on high for 4 hours.

Serve and enjoy.

Calories 636, Fat 17.9 g, Carbohydrates 113.6 g, Sugar 54.1 g, Protein 8.7 g, Cholesterol 0 mg

Chef Marino

Vegetarian Chili Bowl

Total Time: 4 hours 20 minutes

Serves: 8

Ingredients

1 tsp garam masala
4 large tomatoes, peeled, seeded and chopped
1/3 cup can black beans, drained and rinsed
1/3 cup can chickpea, rinsed and drained
1 1/2 cups onions, chopped
1 cup green bell peppers, chopped
3 garlic cloves, minced
1/3 cup can red beans, rinsed and drained
1 1/2 cup vegetable stock
2 tbsp fresh cilantro, chopped
2 tbsp vegetable oil
2 green chili, minced
1/2 medium zucchini, cut into pieces
1 cup celery, chopped
1/2 tbsp chili powder
1/2 tbsp ground coriander
1/2 tsp cumin powder
1 tsp dried oregano
1 tsp dried thyme
1 tsp fresh ginger
1/4 tsp turmeric
1 1/4 tsp salt

Directions

Heat oil in the pan over medium heat.

Add onion, celery, green chilies, and ginger into the pan and
sauté for 5 minutes.

Add spices and stir for another 2 minutes.

Add remaining all ingredients into the slow cooker along with pan mixture. stir well.

Cover and cook on low for 8 hours.

Serve and enjoy.

Calories 135, Fat 5.7 g, Carbohydrates 19.5 g, Sugar 6.7 g, Protein 4.4 g, Cholesterol 0 mg

Chef Marino

Healthy Turmeric Lentil Bean Chili

Total Time: 4 hours 15 minutes

Serves: 6

Ingredients

15 oz can red beans, rinsed and drained
1 cup coconut milk
1 tsp turmeric
1 tsp chili powder
1 tsp ground cumin
6 oz can tomato paste
2 cups water
32 oz vegetable stock
1 small onion, chopped
2 cups green lentils, rinsed and drained

Directions

Add all ingredients except coconut milk into the slow cooker and stir well.

Cover and cook on high for 4 hours.

Add coconut milk and stir well.

Stir well and serve.

Calories 598, Fat 11.5 g, Carbohydrates 92.6 g, Sugar 9.2 g, Protein 35.5 g, Cholesterol 0 mg

Chickpea Kale Sweet Potato Stew

Total Time: 4 hours 20 minutes

Serves: 8

Ingredients

15.5 oz can chickpeas, drained and rinsed
5 oz kale, chopped
2 red bell peppers, diced
1 1/2 lbs sweet potatoes, peeled and cut into pieces
2 tbsp curry powder
1 tsp fresh ginger, peeled and minced
3 garlic cloves, minced
2 cups vegetable broth
14.5 oz can tomatoes, drained and diced
1/4 tsp black pepper
14 oz can coconut milk
1 tsp vegetable oil
1 large onion, diced
1 tbsp kosher salt

Directions

Heat oil in the pan over medium heat.

Add onion and 1 tsp salt and sauté for 5 minutes.

Add potatoes and 1 tsp salt and sauté for another 5 minutes.

Add curry powder, garlic, and ginger and stir for 2 minutes.

Add pan mixture into the slow cooker along with remaining
ingredients except for kale and coconut milk.

Cover and cook on high for 4 hours.

Add coconut milk and kale and stir well. Cook for another 10 minutes.

Serve and enjoy.

Calories 323, Fat 12.6 g, Carbohydrates 47.7 g, Sugar 4.7 g, Protein 8 g, Cholesterol 0 mg

Chickpea Spinach Cauliflower Curry

Total Time: 6 hours 15 minutes

Serves: 6

Ingredients

2 cups baby spinach, chopped
15 oz can chickpeas
1/2 tbsp curry powder
1 tbsp garam masala
1 cup vegetable broth
14 oz can coconut milk
1 sweet potato, peeled and diced
2 cups cauliflower florets
2 cups can tomatoes, chopped
1 tbsp ginger, minced
1 garlic clove, minced
1/2 onion, chopped
1 tsp vegetable oil
1 tsp salt

Directions

Heat oil in the pan over medium heat.

Add ginger, garlic, and onion to the pan and sauté for 5 minutes.

Add pan mixture into the slow cooker with remaining

ingredients except for spinach.

Cover and cook on low for 6 hours.

Add spinach and stir well.

Serve with rice and enjoy.

Calories 282, Fat 16.1 g, Carbohydrates 30.1 g, Sugar 5.3 g, Protein 8 g, Cholesterol 0 mg

Indian Cookbook

Spicy Winter Chickpeas

Total Time: 6 hours 15 minutes

Serves: 4

Ingredients

1 1/2 cups dried chickpeas, rinsed and drained

2 tbsp parsley, chopped

1 tbsp lemon juice

1 bay leaf

1/2 butternut squash, cut into 1-inch cubes

10 green olive, pitted

1 tsp tamarind paste

2 garlic cloves, minced

2 tomatoes, diced

1 large onion, chopped

2 tbsp vegetable oil

1/2 tsp ground black pepper

1 tsp curry powder

1 tsp ground ginger

1 tsp garam masala

1 tsp smoked paprika

1 tsp turmeric

1/2 tsp salt

Directions

Heat oil in the pan over medium heat.

Add garlic, ginger, and onion to the pan and sauté for 5 minutes.

Add spices and sauté for 1 minute. Transfer mixture into the
slow cooker.

Add remaining ingredients into the slow cooker and stir well.

Cover and cook on low for 6 hours.

Serve and enjoy.

Calories 425, Fat 14.3 g, Carbohydrates 60.5 g, Sugar 12.6 g, Protein 16.3 g, Cholesterol 0 mg

Spicy Curried Chickpeas

Total Time: 6 hours 20 minutes

Serves: 4

Ingredients

1.1 lbs chickpeas, rinsed and drained
1/2 tsp dried herbs
1/2 tsp nutmeg
1/2 tsp garam masala
1/2 tsp coriander powder
1 tsp tomato puree
14 oz tomatoes, chopped
2 garlic cloves, minced
2 onion, chopped
1 tsp cumin seeds
4 tsp vegetable oil
2 bay leaves
Salt

Directions

Soaked chickpeas in a water for overnight.

Heat oil in the pan over medium heat.

Add cumin seeds, garlic, and onion into the pan and sauté for 5 minutes.

Add tomato paste, tomatoes and spices and sauté for 2 minutes.

Transfer pan mixture into the blender and blend until smooth.

Add chickpeas, bay leaves, and blended puree into the slow cooker and stir well.

Cover and cook on low for 6 hours.

Serve with rice and enjoy.

Calories 540, Fat 12.6 g, Carbohydrates 85.7 g, Sugar 18.5 g, Protein 25.8 g, Cholesterol 0 mg

Spiced Green Peas Rice

Total Time: 2 hours 20 minutes

Serves: 6

Ingredients

1 cup green peas
2 tsp chili powder
2 tomatoes, pureed
1 tsp turmeric powder
2 green chilies, chopped
1 tsp cumin seeds
1 tbsp vegetable oil
2 potatoes, peeled and chopped
1 cup basmati rice, rinsed and drained
2 cups water

Directions

Add water, rice, and potatoes into the slow cooker. Heat oil in the pan over medium heat. Add cumin seeds, turmeric, chili powder, tomato puree, green chilies, and salt to the pan and sauté for 2 minutes. Transfer pan mixture into the slow cooker and stir well. Cover and cook on high for 1 1/2 hours. Add green peas and cook for another 30 minutes. Serve and enjoy.

Calories 214, Fat 3 g, Carbohydrates 41.8 g, Sugar 3.4 g, Protein 5.3 g, Cholesterol 0 mg

Buttered Peas Rice

Total Time: 2 hours 15 minutes

Serves: 4

Ingredients

1 cup brown rice, uncooked
2 tbsp green onion, sliced
1 cup frozen peas
1 bell pepper, chopped
2 tbsp butter
1 1/4 cup water
Pepper
Salt

Directions

Add all ingredients into the slow cooker and mix well.

Cover and cook on high for 2 hours.

Serve and enjoy.

Calories 265, Fat 7.2 g, Carbohydrates 44.4 g, Sugar 3.4 g, Protein 6 g, Cholesterol 15 mg

VEGETABLE RECIPES

Delicious Spiced Potatoes and Cauliflower
Total Time: 4 hours 15 minutes
Serves: 8

Ingredients
large cauliflower head, cut into florets
1 large potato, peeled and diced
1 tsp fresh ginger, grated
2 cloves garlic, minced
2 jalapeno peppers, sliced
1 medium onion, peeled and diced
1 medium tomato, diced
1 tbsp cumin seeds
1 tsp turmeric
3 tbsp vegetable oil
1 tbsp fresh cilantro, chopped
1/4 tsp cayenne pepper
1 tbsp garam masala
1 tbsp kosher salt

Directions
Add all ingredients except cilantro into the slow cooker and mix well.

Chef Marino

Cover and cook on low for 4 hours.

Garnish with cilantro and serve.

Calories 123, Fat 5.6 g, Carbohydrates 16.7 g, Sugar 4 g, Protein 3.6 g, Cholesterol 0 mg

Scrumptious Spinach Paneer

Total Time: 5 hours 15 minutes

Serves: 6

Ingredients

12 oz paneer cheese

8 oz fresh spinach, chopped

30 oz frozen spinach, thawed

14 oz can coconut milk

1/8 tsp cayenne pepper

1 tbsp ground cumin

1 tbsp ground coriander

1 tbsp garam masala

1 1/2 cups can tomato sauce

3 tbsp fresh ginger, minced

4 garlic cloves, chopped

1 tsp salt

Directions

Add all ingredients except fresh spinach and paneer into the slow cooker.

Cover and cook on low for 3 hours.

Add fresh spinach and cook for 1 hour.

Using immersion blender blend mixture until smooth.

Add paneer cheese and cook for 1 hour.

Serve and enjoy.

Calories 220, Fat 10 g, Carbohydrates 16 g, Sugar 6 g, Protein 20 g, Cholesterol 0 mg

Chef Marino

Tasty Spinach Potato

Total Time: 3 hours 15 minutes
Serves: 4

Ingredients

1 1/2 lbs potatoes, peel and cut into chunks
1/2 lb fresh spinach, chopped
1/2 tsp chili powder
1/2 tsp garam masala
1/2 tsp ground coriander
1/2 tsp cumin
1 tbsp vegetable oil
1/4 cup water
1/2 onion, sliced
Pepper
Salt

Directions

Add all ingredients into the slow cooker and stir well.

Cover and cook on low for 3 hours.

Serve and enjoy.

Calories 168, Fat 3.9 g, Carbohydrates 30.4 g, Sugar 2.8 g, Protein 4.7 g, Cholesterol 0 mg

Spicy Eggplant Potatoes

Total Time: 2 hours 40 minutes

Serves: 8

Ingredients

2 medium eggplants, cut into 1-inch cubes
1 large potato, peeled and cut into 1/2 inch cubes
2 jalapeño chilies, seeded and minced
1 tbsp ground cumin
1 tbsp chili powder
1 medium onion, chopped
1 tsp ginger, grated
6 garlic cloves, minced
1 tbsp garam masala
1 tsp turmeric
2 tbsp fresh cilantro, chopped
1/4 cup vegetable oil
1 tbsp kosher salt

Directions

Add all ingredients into the slow cooker and stir well.

Cover and cook on high for 2 hours.

Remove lid and cook on low for another 30 minutes.

Serve and enjoy.

Calories 147, Fat 7.5 g, Carbohydrates 19.4 g, Sugar 5.2 g, Protein 2.9 g, Cholesterol 0 mg

Healthy Vegetable Coconut Curry

Total Time: 4 hours 20 minutes
Serves: 8

Ingredients

1/4 cup cilantro, chopped
1 cup green peas
1 1/2 cups carrots, peeled and cut into strips
14 oz can coconut milk
1 oz dry onion soup mix
2 bell pepper, cut into strips
1/2 tsp cayenne pepper
1/2 tsp red pepper flakes
1 tbsp chili powder
2 tbsp flour
1/4 cup curry powder
5 potatoes, peeled and cut into cubes
Water as needed

Directions

Add all ingredients into the slow cooker and mix well.
Cover and cook on low for 4 hours.
Stir well and serve.

Indian Cookbook

Calories 370, Fat 18.3 g, Carbohydrates 48.8 g, Sugar 5.4 g, Protein 8.2 g, Cholesterol 0 mg

Easy Whole Cauliflower Curry

Total Time: 4 hours 15 minutes
Serves: 4

Ingredients

1 large cauliflower head, trimmed
2 garlic cloves, sliced
1/2 onion, chopped
2 small potatoes, quartered
1 red pepper, sliced
For sauce:
1/2 tsp cayenne pepper
1 tsp cumin
2 tbsp curry powder
2 cups can coconut milk
2 cups vegetable broth

Directions

Add red pepper, potatoes, onion, garlic, and cauliflower into the slow cooker.
In a bowl, whisk together all sauce ingredients and pour over cauliflower.
Cover and cook on low for 4 hours.
About 15 minutes before serving add coconut milk and stir well. Serve and enjoy.

Calories 383, Fat 25.8 g, Carbohydrates 34.3 g, Sugar 8.6 g, Protein 11.4 g, Cholesterol 0 mg

Chef Marino

Vegetable Curried Rice

Total Time: 4 hours 10 minutes
Serves: 4

Ingredients

1 1/2 cups green cabbage, chopped
2 cups mushrooms, chopped
1 cup broccoli, chopped
1 cup brown rice
1 tsp curry powder
2 tbsp apple cider vinegar
1/4 tsp dried thyme
1/2 tsp garlic powder
1/2 tsp black pepper
4 cups vegetable broth
1 tsp salt

Directions

Add all ingredients into the slow cooker and mix well.

Cover and cook on low for 4 hours.

Using fork fluff the rice.

Serve and enjoy.

Calories 237, Fat 2.9 g, Carbohydrates 42.1 g, Sugar 2.7 g, Protein 10.7 g, Cholesterol 0 mg

Curried Zucchini Eggplant

Total Time: 4 hours 15 minutes

Serves: 4

Ingredients

4 cups zucchini, chopped
4 cups eggplant, peeled and chopped
1/4 cup vegetable broth
15 oz can coconut milk
6 oz can tomato paste
1/4 tsp cumin
1/4 tsp cayenne pepper
1 tbsp garam masala
1 tbsp curry powder
4 garlic cloves, minced
1 onion, chopped
1 tsp salt

Directions

Add all ingredients into the slow cooker and mix well.

Cover and cook on low for 4 hours.

Stir well and serve with rice.

Calories 307, Fat 23.6 g, Carbohydrates 24.3 g, Sugar 10.9 g, Protein 7.2 g, Cholesterol 0 mg

Chef Marino

Flavourful Vegetable Korma

Total Time: 5 hours 15 minutes

Serves: 4

Ingredients

2 tbsp almond meal

1 tbsp red pepper flakes

1 tsp garam masala

2 tbsp curry powder

10 oz coconut milk

2 garlic cloves, minced

1/2 large onion, chopped

1 cup green beans, chopped

1/2 cup frozen green peas

2 large carrots, chopped

1 large cauliflower head, cut into florets

1 tsp sea salt

Directions

Add all ingredients into the slow cooker and stir well.

Cover and cook on high for 5 hours.

Serve and enjoy.

Calories 295, Fat 19.4 g, Carbohydrates 28.7 g, Sugar 11.8 g, Protein 9.1 g, Cholesterol 0 mg

Potato Okra Curry

Total Time: 3 hours 15 minutes

Serves: 6

Ingredients

1 1/2 lbs potatoes, peeled and cut into pieces
1 lb okra, cut the ends and sliced
2 cups vegetable stock
13 oz can coconut milk
1 1/2 tbsp curry powder
3/4 tsp red pepper flakes
2 tsp fresh ginger, grated
4 garlic cloves, minced
1 large onion, chopped
1 1/2 tbsp vegetable oil
1 bell pepper, seeded and chopped
1 1/2 tsp salt

Directions

Add potatoes, bell pepper, and okra into the slow cooker. Heat oil in a pan over medium heat.
Add garlic, onion, and ginger to the pan and sauté for 5 minutes. Remove pan from heat and stir in spices.
Transfer pan mixture into the slow cooker and stir well.
Cover and cook on low for 3 hours.
Stir well and serve with rice.

Calories 290, Fat 17.8 g, Carbohydrates 31.8 g, Sugar 5.3 g, Protein 5.5 g, Cholesterol 0 mg

Delicious Navratan Korma

Total Time: 8 hours 15 minutes
Serves: 4

Ingredients

1 cup cauliflower florets
1/2 cup tomatoes, diced
1/2 cup green peas
1 cup carrots, chopped
2 tbsp sour cream
1/4 cup coconut milk
1 tbsp raisins
1/4 tsp chili powder
1/2 tsp ground coriander
1/2 tsp ground turmeric
1 tbsp ginger, grated
2 tbsp bell pepper, minced
1/4 onion, chopped
1/2 cup water
Salt

Directions

Add all ingredients except sour cream into the slow cooker and stir well.
Cover and cook on low for 8 hours.
Stir in sour cream and serve with rice.

Calories 118, Fat 5.3 g, Carbohydrates 16.8 g, Sugar 8.8 g, Protein 3.4 g, Cholesterol 3 mg

Slow Cooker Sambar

Total Time: 6 hours 10 minutes

Serves: 2

Ingredients

1/4 cup pink lentils

1 cup water

1/2 tsp tamarind paste

1 tsp sambar powder

4 curry leaves

1/4 cup tomatoes, chopped

1/4 cup eggplants, cut into pieces

1/4 cup pumpkin, cut into pieces

1 medium onion, sliced

1 drumstick, peeled and cut into pieces

Salt

Directions

Add all ingredients into the slow cooker and stir well.

Cover and cook on low for 6 hours.

Stir well and serve hot with rice.

Calories 130, Fat 0.6 g, Carbohydrates 24.7 g, Sugar 5.3 g, Protein 7.5 g, Cholesterol 0 mg

Chef Marino

Creamy Carrot Squash Soup

Total Time: 6 hours 15 minutes
Serves: 8

Ingredients

1 lb butternut squash, peeled and diced
1/2 lb carrots, peeled and cut into chunks
13.5 oz can coconut milk
1/4 tsp ground sage
1 tsp pepper
1 bay leaf
3 cups vegetable broth
1 apple, peeled and sliced
1 medium onion, diced
1 tsp salt

Directions

Add squash, bay leaf, apple, carrots, onion, and broth into the slow cooker.
Cover and cook on low for 6 hours.
Discard bay leaf and using immersion blender blend until smooth.
Add coconut milk, sage, pepper, and salt. Stir well.
Serve and enjoy.

Calories 163, Fat 11.3 g, Carbohydrates 15.8 g, Sugar 5.1 g, Protein 3.8 g, Cholesterol 0 mg

Yummy Slow Cooked Potatoes

Total Time: 6 hours 15 minutes

Serves: 4

Ingredients

2.2 lbs potatoes, peel and cut into cubes
1/2 tsp chili powder
1/2 tsp cumin
1 1/2 tsp turmeric
1 tsp garam masala
1 tsp ground ginger
1 tsp mustard seeds
4 tomatoes, chopped
1/4 tsp red chili flakes
1 tbsp vegetable oil
1 tsp salt

Directions

In a bowl, mix together chili flakes, chili powder, cumin,
turmeric, garam masala, and ginger.

Heat oil in the pan over medium heat.

Add mustard seeds into the pan and stir until they start to pop then add onion and sauté until lightly brown.

Add mixed spices and stir for a minute.

Add tomatoes and salt and stir for a minute.

Place potatoes in the slow cooker then pour pan mixture over the potatoes.

Cover and cook on low for 6 hours.

Stir well and serve.

Calories 235, Fat 4.4 g, Carbohydrates 45.8 g, Sugar 6.2 g, Protein 5.7 g, Cholesterol 0 mg

Curried Potatoes

Total Time: 6 hours 15 minutes

Serves: 6

Ingredients

7 potatoes, washed and cut into chunks

2 tsp sugar

2 tsp chili powder

2 tsp curry powder

2 tsp paprika

14.5 oz can tomatoes, diced

1 tbsp vegetable oil

1/2 tsp kosher salt

Directions

Add all ingredients into the slow cooker and stir well.

Cover and cook on low for 6 hours.

Serve and enjoy.

Calories 218, Fat 2.9 g, Carbohydrates 45.1 g, Sugar 6.7 g, Protein 5.1 g, Cholesterol 0 mg

Chef Marino

Mushroom Eggplant Potato Curry

Total Time: 4 hours 15 minutes

Serves: 6

Ingredients

8 mushrooms, quartered
1 large eggplant, peeled and cut into 1-inch pieces
3 potatoes, peeled and cut into 1/2 inch cubes
1 bay leaf
2 tsp fresh ginger, grated
14 oz can tomatoes, chopped
1/2 cup red pepper, chopped
1 tsp black pepper
1 tbsp ground cumin
2 garlic cloves, minced
1 large onion, chopped
2 tbsp vegetable oil
1 tsp lime juice
Salt

Directions

Heat oil in the pan over medium heat.

Add eggplant to the pan and sauté until lightly brown.

Transfer eggplant to the slow cooker.

In the same pan, add onion and sauté for 3 minutes. Add garlic, pepper, and cumin and sauté for a minute.

Transfer onion mixture to the slow cooker along with remaining all ingredients and stir well.

Cover and cook on high for 4 hours.

Stir well and serve.

Calories 173, Fat 5.3 g, Carbohydrates 29.4 g, Sugar 6.7 g, Protein 4.6 g, Cholesterol 0 mg

E

Chef Marino

ggplant Chickpea Curry

Total Time: 8 hours 40 minutes

Serves: 6

Ingredients

15 oz can chickpeas, rinsed and drained
1 tbsp fresh ginger, minced
2 tsp cumin
1 tbsp garam masala
1 tbsp curry powder
3 cups vegetable broth
15 oz can tomatoes
4 garlic cloves, minced
3 lbs eggplant, diced
2 cups onion, diced
2 tsp salt

Directions

Add all ingredients except chickpeas into the slow cooker.

Cover and cook on low for 8 hours.

Add chickpeas and cook for another 30 minutes.

Stir well and serve.

Calories 203, Fat 2.3 g, Carbohydrates 39.2 g, Sugar 11.3 g, Protein 9.7 g, Cholesterol 0 mg

Coconut Eggplant Curry

Total Time: 4 hours 10 minutes

Serves: 6

Ingredients

2 lbs eggplant, cut into 1 inch cubed
4 garlic cloves, minced
14.5 oz can coconut milk
6 oz tomato paste
1 tbsp curry powder
1 medium onion, chopped
1 green bell pepper, seeded and chopped
2 Serrano peppers, seeded and minced
1 tbsp garam masala
1 tsp salt

Directions

Add all ingredients into the slow cooker and stir well.

Cover and cook on low for 4 hours.

Serve and enjoy.

Calories 216, Fat 15.2 g, Carbohydrates 20.7 g, Sugar 9.8 g, Protein 4.8 g, Cholesterol 0 mg

Chef Marino

Creamy Cauliflower Soup

Total Time: 4 hours 20 minutes
Serves: 6

Ingredients

1 cauliflower head
2 cups vegetable broth
3 garlic cloves
1/4 cup dried cranberries
1/4 cup pine nuts
13.5 oz can coconut milk
5.3 oz plain yogurt
1 tbsp curry powder
1 tbsp water
3/4 tsp garam masala
1/2 cup sugar
1/2 tsp salt

Directions

Add cauliflower, broth, and garlic into the slow cooker. Cover and cook on low for 4 hours.

Add cauliflower mixture into the blender along with yogurt and coconut milk and blend until smooth.

Pour into the six serving bowls.

In a pan, cook over medium heat pine nuts with water, garam masala, and sugar. Cook until sugar is crystallized.

Sprinkle pan mixture over the soup.

Serve and enjoy.

Calories 276, Fat 18.5 g, Carbohydrates 25.1 g, Sugar 20.1 g, Protein 6.2 g, Cholesterol 2 mg

Chef Marino

Delicious Sweet Potato Curry

Total Time: 6 hours 15 minutes

Serves: 6

Ingredients

1 sweet potato, diced
1 courgette, diced
1/4 cup cashew nuts
14 oz can tomatoes, chopped
1 tsp curry powder
1/2 tsp chili powder
1/2 tsp black pepper
2 tbsp tomato puree
4 tbsp flour
14 oz can coconut milk
1 tsp garlic, minced
2 onions, diced
4 tomatoes, diced
1 tsp ginger, minced
2 tsp garam masala
1 tbsp vegetable oil

Directions

Heat oil in the pan over medium heat.

Add ginger, onion, and garlic to the pan and sauté for 5 minutes.

Add tomato paste, flour, and spices and cook for a minute.

Add coconut milk and stir well and cook until thickened.

Transfer pan mixture into the slow cooker along with remaining ingredients and mix well.

Cover and cook on low for 6 hours.

Serve and enjoy.

Calories 275, Fat 19.5 g, Carbohydrates 24 g, Sugar 8.3 g, Protein 5.5 g, Cholesterol 0 mg

Chef Marino

Flavorful Vegetable Curry

Total Time: 7 hours 15 minutes

Serves: 4

Ingredients

15 oz can chickpeas, rinsed and drained
8 oz fresh green beans, cut into 1-inch pieces
4 medium carrots, sliced
2 medium potatoes, cut into 1/2 inch cubes
1 cup onion, chopped
14 oz can vegetable broth
14 oz can tomatoes, diced
2 tbsp tapioca
2 tsp curry powder
1 tsp ground coriander
3 garlic cloves, minced
1/8 tsp ground cinnamon
1/4 tsp red pepper, crushed
1/4 tsp salt

Directions

Add all ingredients into the slow cooker and stir well. Cover and cook on low for 7 hours.

Stir well and serve with rice.

Calories 367, Fat 3.1 g, Carbohydrates 75.3 g Sugar 11.8 g, Protein 12.6 g, Cholesterol 1 mg

Delicious Tofu Coconut Curry

Total Time: 4 hours 15 minutes

Serves: 4

Ingredients

1 cup firm tofu, diced
2 tsp garlic cloves, minced
1 cup onion, chopped
8 oz tomato paste
2 cups bell pepper, chopped
1 tbsp garam masala
2 tbsp butter
1 tbsp curry powder
10 oz can coconut milk
1 1/2 tsp sea salt

Directions

Add all ingredients into the slow cooker and stir well.

Cover and cook on low for 4 hours.

Stir well and serve with rice.

Calories 179, Fat 9.1 g, Carbohydrates 20.4 g, Sugar 11.6 g, Protein 8.9 g, Cholesterol 15 mg

Chef Marino

Creamy Coconut Pumpkin Curry

Total Time: 6 hours 15 minutes

Serves: 6

Ingredients

15 oz can coconut milk, unsweetened
2 cups pumpkin puree
1 cup vegetable stock
3 carrots, cut into 1-inch pieces
3 cups sweet potatoes, cut into 1-inch cubes
1/2 tbsp curry powder
1/4 tsp turmeric powder
1/4 tsp ground black pepper
1/2 large onion, diced
1 garlic clove, minced
2 chicken breasts, cut into 1-inch cubes
1 lime juice
2 tsp garam masala
1/2 tsp kosher salt

Directions

Add all ingredients into the slow cooker and mix well. Cover and cook on low for 6 hours.

Serve with rice and enjoy.

Calories 357, Fat 17.7 g, Carbohydrates 35 g, Sugar 7.4 g, Protein 17.6 g, Cholesterol 43 mg

Hearty Potato Curry

Total Time: 8 hours 10 minutes
Serves: 4

Ingredients

1 lb potatoes, cut into 1-inch cubes
1/2 tsp cumin
1/2 tsp coriander
1/2 tsp peppercorns
1 cinnamon stick
1 cups vegetable stock
1 tsp tamarind paste
1 bay leaf
1/4 tsp red pepper, crushed
1/2 tsp garam masala
4 garlic cloves, minced
2 tsp ginger, minced
1 onion, diced
2 tbsp vegetable oil
1 1/2 tsp paprika
1 1/2 tsp turmeric
1/2 cup frozen peas
2 cups coconut milk
2 tbsp all purpose flour
Pepper
Salt

Directions

Heat 1 tbsp oil in the pan over medium heat.

Add onion and cook until golden brown, about 3 minutes.

Add powder spices and stir for 1 minute.

Transfer onion mixture to the blender with tamarind, ginger, garlic, and coconut milk and blend until smooth.

Pour blended mixture into the slow cooker with remaining ingredients except for peas and flour.

Cover and cook on low for 8 hours.

Add peas and stir well. Whisk flour in little water and pour into the slow cooker.

Stir well and serve.

Calories 476, Fat 36.5 g, Carbohydrates 37.2 g, Sugar 8.8 g, Protein 7 g, Cholesterol 0 mg

Mix Vegetable Curry

Total Time: 6 hours 10 minutes
Serves: 4

Ingredients

3 1/2 cups broccoli florets
2.5 oz green beans
2 medium carrots, peeled and sliced
2 large sweet potatoes, diced
3 tbsp tomato puree
14 oz can coconut milk
1 red chili, seeded and chopped
1 tsp garam masala
1 tsp ground turmeric
2 tsp ground coriander
2 tsp ground cumin
1 tsp chili powder
1 tsp ginger, grated
1 tsp garlic, grated
1 onion, diced

Directions

Add all ingredients except green beans into the slow cooker and mix well. Cover and cook on low for 5 hours. Add green beans and stir well and cook for another 1 hour. Serve with rice.

Calories 313, Fat 22 g, Carbohydrates 28.3 g, Sugar 5.1 g, Protein 6.3 g, Cholesterol 0 mg

MEAT RECIPES

Tasty Chicken Tikka Masala

Total Time: 6 hours 25 minutes

Serves: 6

Ingredients

2 lbs chicken thighs, skinless and boneless, cut into 2-inch pieces
10 oz frozen peas, thawed
1 1/2 cups heavy cream
1 tbsp cornstarch
1 tbsp sugar
28 oz can tomatoes
1 tsp ginger, grated
3 tbsp garam masala
1/2 tsp red pepper flakes
6 garlic cloves, minced
1 large onion, diced
2 tbsp vegetable oil
1 cup plain yogurt
1 tbsp ground cumin
1 tbsp ground coriander
1 tsp kosher salt

Directions

In a large bowl, combine together chicken, yogurt, cumin,
ground coriander, and salt. Marinade for 10 minutes.

Heat 1 tbsp oil in the pan over medium-high heat.

Place marinated chicken into the pan and cook until lightly brown on both the sides.
Transfer chicken into the slow cooker.

In the same pan, heat remaining oil. Add onions, red pepper flakes, and garlic and saute fo
r 5 minutes.
Add ginger, garam masala, and salt and cook for 1 minute.
Add sugar and tomatoes, turn heat to high and bring to boil. Transfer into the slow cooker.
Cover and cook on low for 6 hours.

Whisk together 1/4 cup heavy cream and cornstarch and add to the slow cooker along with remaining peas and heavy cream.

Stir to mix and cover and cook for another 10 minutes.
Serve and enjoy.

Calories 557, Fat 27.8 g, Carbohydrates 24.5 g, Sugar 12.7 g, Protein 51.1 g, Cholesterol 178 mg

Chef Marino

Delicious Chicken Tandoori

Total Time: 8 hours 20 minutes

Serves: 4

Ingredients

14 oz coconut milk
4 chicken thighs
1 tsp fresh ginger, grated
1 tsp paprika
1 tsp cayenne pepper
2 tsp tomato paste
2 tsp garam masala
1 tsp ground coriander
1 tsp ground cumin

Directions

Add all ingredients into the slow cooker and mix well.

Cover and cook on low for 8 hours.

Serve and enjoy.

Calories 514, Fat 34.8 g, Carbohydrates 7.1 g, Sugar 3.8 g, Protein 44.9 g, Cholesterol 130 mg

Indian Cookbook

Peanut Butter Chicken

Total Time: 4 hours 30 minutes

Serves: 6

Ingredients

3 chicken breasts, skinless and boneless
1 tbsp lime juice
2 tbsp cornstarch
3 garlic cloves, minced
1 tbsp ginger, minced
1 tbsp rice wine vinegar
2 tbsp honey
2 tbsp soy sauce
1/3 cup creamy peanut butter
1 cup coconut milk

Directions

Add all ingredients except lime juice and cornstarch into the slow cooker and mix well.
Cover and cook on low for 4 hours.
Whisk together cornstarch and 2 tbsp water and pour into the slow cooker.
Stir well and cook for another 20 minutes until gravy thickens.
Serve and enjoy.

Calories 356, Fat 22.2 g, Carbohydrates 15.4 g, Sugar 8.7 g, Protein 26.2 g, Cholesterol 65 mg

Chef Marino

Spicy Chicken Curry

Total Time: 6 hours 20 minutes

Serves: 4

Ingredients

4 chicken thighs, boneless and cut into chunks
3 tbsp flour
2 tsp ground coriander
2 tsp garam masala
2 tsp turmeric
2 tsp ground cumin
1 tsp ginger, grated
1/2 lemon juice
4 garlic cloves, crushed
2 onion, chopped
2 green chilies, chopped
14 oz can tomatoes, chopped
1 tbsp vegetable oil

Directions

Add ginger, chilies, garlic, and onion into the blender and blend until smooth.

Heat oil in the pan over medium heat.

Add blended puree into the pan and sauté for 3 minutes.

Add spices and sauté for 2-3 minutes.

Add flour and tomatoes into the pan and stir well.

Refill tomato can halfway with water and adds in the pan. Stir well.

Add chicken into the slow cooker and season with pepper and salt.

Pour pan mixture over the chicken with lemon juice.

Cover and cook on low for 6 hours.

Serve and enjoy.

Calories 387, Fat 14.8 g, Carbohydrates 17.3 g, Sugar 6 g, Protein 44.9 g, Cholesterol 130 mg

Chef Marino

Juicy and Tender Goat Curry

Total Time: 5 hours 15 minutes
Serves: 6

Ingredients

2 lbs goat meat
2 Serrano pepper, minced
1 tsp paprika
1 tsp chili powder
1 tsp turmeric powder
1 tsp cumin powder
1 tbsp coriander powder
2 cardamom pods
2 garlic cloves, minced
1 tbsp ghee
1 bay leaf
3 whole cloves
1 tsp fresh ginger, minced
1 large onion, chopped
1 cup water
1 tsp garam masala
28 oz can tomatoes, diced
2 tsp salt

Directions

Add cardamom and cloves into the grinder and grind well.

Add all ingredients into the slow cooker except water, garam masala, and tomatoes.

Cover and cook on high for 4 hours.

Add water, garam masala, and tomatoes and stir well.

Cook for another 1 hour until meat is tender.

Serve and enjoy.

Calories 230, Fat 5.9 g, Carbohydrates 10.6 g, Sugar 5.8 g, Protein 33.6 g, Cholesterol 92 mg

Chef Marino

Delicious Slow Cooked Beef

Total Time: 6 hours 15 minutes

Serves: 4

Ingredients

2 lbs beef chuck steak, diced
1/2 cup coriander, chopped
2 cardamom pods
1 cinnamon stick
14 oz can tomatoes, diced
1/4 cup curry paste
1 red chili, chopped
1 tsp ginger, grated
2 garlic cloves, crushed
1 large onion, sliced
2 tbsp vegetable oil
1/4 cup plain flour

Directions

Add beef and flour into the ziplock bag and shake well.

Heat oil in the saucepan over medium heat.

Add beef into the saucepan and cook for 3-4 minutes or until lightly brown. Transfer beef into the slow cooker.

In the same pan, add onion, ginger, and garlic and sauté for 4 minutes.

Add curry paste and chili and stir for 1 minute.

Add 3/4 cup water, tomatoes, cardamom, and cinnamon and stir well. Transfer mixture into the slow cooker.

Cover and cook on low for 5 1/2 hours or until beef is tender.

Add coriander and stir well.

Serve and enjoy.

Calories 651, Fat 29.9 g, Carbohydrates 19.7 g, Sugar 5 g, Protein 71.8 g, Cholesterol 203 mg

Simple Beef Curry

Total Time: 8 hours 40 minutes
Serves: 4

Ingredients

12 oz beef steak, cut into 1-inch pieces
2 onions, chopped
14 oz can tomatoes, chopped
2 tsp garam masala
4 garlic cloves, chopped
4 tsp ground cumin
4 tsp ground coriander
2 tsp ground turmeric
2 chilies, chopped
1 tsp ginger, grated
7 oz yogurt
4 tbsp vegetable oil

Directions

Heat oil in the pan over medium heat.

Add beef to the pan and cook for 4-5 minutes or until lightly brown. Transfer beef into the slow cooker.

In the same pan, sauté onion, ginger, chili, and garlic for 2 minutes.

Add spices and stir-fry for 1 minute. Transfer pan mixture to the slow cooker.

Add remaining ingredients except for yogurt into the slow cooker and stir well.

Cover and cook on low for 8 hours.

Add yogurt and stir well and cook for another 30 minutes.

Serve and enjoy.

Calories 375, Fat 20.2 g, Carbohydrates 16.7 g, Sugar 9.3 g, Protein 30.8 g, Cholesterol 79 mg

Chef Marino

Easy Curried Chicken

Total Time: 4 hours 15 minutes

Serves: 4

Ingredients

2 tbsp tomato paste
14 oz can coconut milk
3 garlic cloves, minced
2 tbsp fresh ginger, minced
1 tsp cumin
1 tsp turmeric
1 tsp garam masala
1 cinnamon stick
2 bay leaves
1 1/2 lbs chicken thighs
1 medium onion, diced
1/4 cup fresh cilantro, chopped
1 1/2 tsp salt

Directions

Add all ingredients into the slow cooker and stir well.
Cover and cook on low for 4 hours.
Using fork shred the meat and stir well into the sauce.

Serve and enjoy.

Calories 553, Fat 34.2 g, Carbohydrates 10.2 g, Sugar 2.3 g, Protein 52.4 g, Cholesterol 151 mg

Chicken Vegetable Curry

Total Time: 3 hours 25 minutes

Serves: 4

Ingredients

2 cups mushrooms, sliced

1 cup green peas

3 chicken breasts, skinless, boneless and cut into pieces

2 tsp ground cayenne

1/2 tsp black pepper

3 tbsp curry powder

1 packet dry onion soup mix

14 oz can coconut milk

10.75 oz can chicken soup

10.75 oz can mushroom soup

1 onion, chopped

1 tbsp butter

Directions

Melt butter in the pan over medium heat. Add onion and cook for 5 minutes. Transfer to the slow cooker.

Add remaining ingredients and stir well.

Cover and cook on high for 1 1/2 hours then reduce heat to low and cook for another 1 1/2 hours.

Serve and enjoy.

Calories 635, Fat 37.9 g, Carbohydrates 32 g, Sugar 2.3 g, Protein 45.2 g, Cholesterol 111 mg

Chef Marino

Spicy Cauliflower Chicken

Total Time: 6 hours 15 minutes

Serves: 4

Ingredients

1 1/2 lbs chicken thighs, skinless, boneless and cut into halves
1 small cauliflower head, cut into florets
1/4 cup raisins
1 onion, chopped
1 tbsp curry powder
2 tbsp ginger, grated
2 tbsp tomato paste
28 oz can tomatoes, diced
1/2 tsp kosher salt

Directions

Add all ingredients into the slow cooker and stir well.

Cover and cook on low for 6 hours.

Serve and enjoy.

Calories 391, Fat 17.3 g, Carbohydrates 26.7 g, Sugar 6.7 g, Protein 31.1 g, Cholesterol 96 mg

Indian Cookbook

Yummy Butter Chicken

Total Time: 4 hours 30 minutes
Serves: 6

Ingredients

4 large chicken thighs, skinless, boneless and cut into pieces
14 oz can coconut milk
1 cup plain yogurt
15 green cardamom pods
6 oz can tomato paste
1 tsp garam masala
2 tsp tandoori masala
1 tsp curry paste
2 tsp curry powder
3 garlic cloves, minced
1 onion, diced
3 tbsp vegetable oil
2 tbsp butter
Salt

Directions

Heat butter and oil in a pan over medium heat.

Add chicken, garlic, and onion to the pan and cook until onion softens.

Stir in tomato paste, garam masala, tandoori masala, curry paste, and curry powder.

Transfer chicken mixture into the slow cooker.

Stir in yogurt, coconut milk, and cardamom pods.

Season with salt.

Cover and cook on high for 4 hours.

Serve and enjoy.

Calories 480, Fat 33.3 g, Carbohydrates 17.2 g, Sugar 7.1 g, Protein 30.6 g, Cholesterol 103 mg

Lamb Curry

Total Time: 8 hours 15 minutes

Serves: 6

Ingredients

2 lbs lamb meat, cut into 1 1/2" cubes
1/4 cup cilantro, chopped
20 almonds
1/4 tsp saffron threads
1 cup plain yogurt
1/2 tsp turmeric
2 large onion, sliced
6 tbsp vegetable oil
3 tomatoes, chopped
1/4 cup dried coconut, unsweetened
5 garlic cloves, crushed
1 tsp fresh ginger, grated
1 tsp garam masala
1 tsp cumin seeds
3 green Chile pepper
4 dried red Chile pepper
Salt

Directions

Add tomatoes, grated coconut, garlic, ginger, garam masala, cumin seeds, green chilies, and red chilies into the blender and blend until smooth.

Heat oil in a pan over medium heat.

Add onion to the pan and sauté for 5 minutes or until softened.

Add spice paste to the pan and cook for 3 minutes.

Stir in meat and salt. Cook over medium heat for 8 minutes.

Mix in almonds, saffron, and yogurt until well combined.

Transfer pan mixture into the slow cooker and stir well.

Cover and cook on low for 8 hours.

Serve and enjoy.

Calories 489, Fat 35.4 g, Carbohydrates 16.1 g, Sugar 7.1 g, Protein 28.1 g, Cholesterol 88 mg

Chicken Quinoa Curry

Total Time: 4 hours 45 minutes

Serves: 6

Ingredients

1 1/2 lbs chicken breast, diced

1/3 cup quinoa

1/4 tsp paprika

1 tbsp curry powder

1/4 cup coconut milk

1 cup chicken broth

1 3/4 cups apples, chopped

1 1/4 cups celery, chopped

3/4 cup onion, chopped

Directions

Add all ingredients except quinoa into the slow cooker and stir well.

Cover and cook on low for 4 hours.

Add quinoa and stir well. Cook for another 35 minutes.

Stir well and serve.

Calories 185, Fat 3.1 g, Carbohydrates 14.4 g, Sugar 8.2 g, Protein 24.4 g, Cholesterol 59 mg

Chef Marino

Delicious Chicken Stew

Total Time: 4 hours 15 minutes

Serves: 8

Ingredients

2 lbs chicken thighs, skinless, boneless and cut into pieces
1 medium onion, chopped
3 garlic cloves, minced
1/4 tsp ground black pepper
15 oz can chickpeas, rinsed and drained
14 oz can tomatoes, diced
1 cup chicken broth
5 tsp curry powder
2 tsp ground ginger
1 bay leaf
1 tbsp vegetable oil
2 tbsp lime juice
1/2 tsp salt

Directions

Add all ingredients into the slow cooker and mix well.
Cover and cook on high for 4 hours.
Serve and enjoy.

Calories 322, Fat 11.1 g, Carbohydrates 17.4 g, Sugar 2.4 g, Protein 36.9 g, Cholesterol 101 mg

Creamy Coconut Chicken Curry

Total Time: 4 hours 15 minutes

Serves: 4

Ingredients

1 lb chicken breasts, skinless and boneless
2 tbsp lemon juice
1 cup green peas
1/2 tsp cayenne
2 tbsp curry powder
15 oz can tomato sauce
1/2 cup chicken stock
1/2 cup coconut milk
2 medium sweet potatoes, diced
15 oz can chickpeas, drained and rinsed
1 medium onion, sliced
1 tsp salt

Directions

Add all ingredients except peas into the slow cooker and mix well.
Cover and cook on high for 4 hours.
Add peas and stir well.
Serve and enjoy.

Calories 579, Fat 17.9 g, Carbohydrates 62.4 g, Sugar 9.5 g, Protein 44.2 g, Cholesterol 101 mg

Chef Marino

Tasty Chicken Kheema

Total Time: 4 hours 20 minutes

Serves: 4

Ingredients

1 lb ground chicken
3/4 cup frozen peas
1 bay leaf
3/4 tsp ground cinnamon
3/4 tsp garam masala
3/4 tsp ground turmeric
3/4 tsp chili powder
3/4 tsp ground cumin
3/4 tsp ground coriander
1 jalapeno, seeded and chopped
4 tbsp cilantro, chopped
3/4 cup can tomato sauce
1 tsp ginger, grated
3 garlic cloves, minced
1 medium onion, chopped
2 tsp butter
1 tsp kosher salt

Directions

Heat butter in a pan over medium heat.

Add onion to the pan and sauté for 5 minutes.

Add ginger and garlic and sauté for 2 minutes.

Add ground chicken and salt and cook for 5 minutes.

Transfer chicken mixture to the slow cooker along with remaining ingredients and stir well.

Cover and cook on high for 4 hours.

Serve and enjoy.

Calories 291, Fat 10.8 g, Carbohydrates 11.8 g, Sugar 4.7 g, Protein 35.8 g, Cholesterol 106 mg

Chef Marino

Shredded Lamb

Total Time: 6 hours 15 minutes
Serves: 6

Ingredients

4.4 lbs lamb shoulder
3 tsp vegetable oil
1 cup chicken stock
1 tbsp ginger, sliced
4 garlic cloves, crushed
2 large onions, sliced
Spice Rub:
1 tsp red chili powder
1 tsp ground coriander
6 peppercorns
1 tsp fennel seeds
1 bay leaf
1 tsp cumin seeds
1 cinnamon stick
6 cloves
1-star anise

Directions

Add allspice rub ingredients into the grinder and grind to coarse powder.

Rub spice powder onto the lamb from both the sides.

Heat oil in the pan over medium-high heat.

Place lamb onto the pan and brown them on both the sides and set aside.

Add remaining ingredients into the slow cooker.

Place lamb into the slow cooker.

Cover and cook on high for 6 hours or until meat is tender.

Remove lamb from slow cooker and using fork shred the meat.

Return shredded meat to the slow cooker and stir well.

Serve with rice and enjoy.

Calories 671, Fat 27.1 g, Carbohydrates 6.7 g, Sugar 2.3 g, Protein 94.4 g, Cholesterol 299 mg

Chef Marino

Yummy Chicken Soup

Total Time: 12 hours 15 minutes

Serves: 6

Ingredients

3 carrots, peeled and sliced
1 tsp ginger, crushed
1/2 tsp garlic, crushed
1/4 tsp turmeric
1/2 onion, diced
12 cups water
5 cloves
2 cinnamon sticks
1/4 tsp black peppercorns
2 chicken breasts
1 lb chicken
1 tbsp sea salt

Directions

Add all ingredients into the slow cooker.
Cover and cook on low for 12 hours.
Remove chicken from slow cooker and using fork shred the chicken.
Return shredded chicken to the slow cooker and stir well. Season with pepper and salt.
Serve and enjoy.

Calories 225, Fat 5.9 g, Carbohydrates 4.3 g, Sugar 1.9 g, Protein 36.4 g, Cholesterol 102 mg

Sweet Beef Curry

Total Time: 8 hours 15 minutes

Serves: 6

Ingredients

2.2 lbs stew beef

1 tbsp raisins

1 tbsp relish

1 tbsp tomato sauce

2 carrots, peeled and chopped

1 onion, chopped

2 celery stalks, chopped

2 apples, chopped

1 tbsp Worcestershire sauce

1/2 cup water

1 tbsp golden syrup

2 tbsp brown sugar

1 tbsp curry powder

2 tsp salt

Directions

Add all ingredients into the slow cooker and mix well. Cover and cook on low for 8 hours.

Serve and enjoy.

Calories 333, Fat 10.3 g, Carbohydrates 23 g, Sugar 15.7 g, Protein 37.4 g, Cholesterol 0 mg

Chef Marino

Yellow Chicken Curry

Total Time: 4 hours 15 minutes

Serves: 6

Ingredients

1 1/2 lbs chicken thighs, boneless, skinless and cut into pieces

1 lb potatoes, diced

1 medium onion, diced

13.5 oz can coconut milk

2 tbsp brown sugar

1 tsp ground turmeric

1 tsp curry powder

2 tsp garlic, minced

1 tbsp fresh ginger, minced

1/2 tsp ground coriander seed

1/2 tsp red pepper

1 tsp kosher salt

Directions

Add all ingredients into the slow cooker and stir well.

Cover and cook on low for 4 hours.

Serve and enjoy.

Calories 296, Fat 8.7 g, Carbohydrates 20.5 g, Sugar 5.1 g, Protein 35.9 g, Cholesterol 101 mg

Spinach Lamb Curry

Total Time: 4 hours 20 minutes

Serves: 8

Ingredients

2 cups plain yogurt
6 cups baby spinach
3 lbs lamb meat, boneless and cut into pieces
2 cups beef broth
1 1/2 tsp ground turmeric
1 1/2 tsp cayenne pepper
2 tsp ground cumin
1 tsp fresh ginger, grated
4 garlic cloves, minced
3 onions, chopped
1/3 cup vegetable oil
Salt

Directions

Heat oil in the pan over medium-high heat.

Add garlic and onions to the pan and sauté for 5 minutes.

Add turmeric, cayenne, cumin, and ginger and sauté for 1 minute.

Add broth to the pan and stir well.

Add meat into the slow cooker with salt.

Pour pan mixture over the meat.

Cover and cook on high for 4 hours.

Just before serving add spinach and cook until wilted, about 5 minutes.

Add yogurt and stir well.

Serve and enjoy.

Calories 479, Fat 23 g, Carbohydrates 10.6 g, Sugar 6.4 g, Protein 53.8 g, Cholesterol 157 mg

Classic Lamb Curry

Total Time: 6 hours 15 minutes
Serves: 6

Ingredients

3.3 lbs lamb, diced
2 bay leaves
2 cardamom pods
1 cinnamon stick
1 cup chicken stock
1 tsp red chili powder
1 tsp paprika
1 tsp garam masala
4 tsp ground cumin
4 tsp ground coriander
1 tsp turmeric
6 garlic cloves, crushed
1 tsp ginger, grated
1 large onion, sliced
3 tbsp vegetable oil
1/4 cup all-purpose flour
Salt

Directions

Add flour and lamb into the large zip-lock bag and shake well and set aside.

Meanwhile, heat 2 tbsp oil in the large frying pan over high heat.

Add lamb to the pan and cook until browned on both the sides, about 7 minutes.

Transfer lamb into the slow cooker.

Heat remaining oil in the pan over medium-high heat.

Add garlic, ginger, and onion to the pan and sauté for 2 minutes.

Add turmeric, red chili powder, paprika, garam masala, cumin, and coriander and sauté for 2 minutes.

Add chicken stock and stir well.

Transfer pan mixture to the slow cooker.

Add bay leaves, cardamom, and cinnamon stick.

Cover and cook on low for 6 hours.

Serve and enjoy.

Calories 568, Fat 25.7 g, Carbohydrates 8.7 g, Sugar 1.3 g, Protein 71.5 g, Cholesterol 225 mg

Easy Lamb Stew

Total Time: 4 hours 15 minutes

Serves: 4

Ingredients

2 lbs lamb, boneless
2 medium onions, chopped
3 garlic cloves, chopped
1 tsp fresh ginger, grated
1 tsp dried mint
2 tbsp vegetable oil
2 tsp ground cumin
2 tsp ground coriander
1 tsp ground turmeric
28 oz can tomatoes, crushed
1.5 tbsp maple syrup
1 tsp garam masala
1 tsp red chili flakes
2 tsp salt

Directions

Heat oil in the pan over medium heat.

Add ginger, garlic, and onion to the pan and sauté for 5 minutes.

Add lamb and cook until browned. Transfer pan mixture into the slow cooker.

Add remaining ingredients and stir well.

Cover and cook on high for 4 hours.

Serve warm and enjoy.

Calories 577, Fat 28.8 g, Carbohydrates 22.2 g, Sugar 13.6 g, Protein 66.5 g, Cholesterol 204 mg

Spicy Beef Roast

Total Time: 5 hours 15 minutes

Serves: 6

Ingredients

2 1/2 lbs beef roast

25 curry leaves

1 tbsp ginger, grated

1 Serrano pepper, minced

2 tbsp lemon juice

2 tbsp garlic, minced

1 tbsp garam masala

1 tsp coriander powder

2 tsp chili powder

1 tsp turmeric

1/2 tsp black pepper

2 onions, chopped

2 tbsp coconut oil

1 tsp mustard seeds

1 tsp salt

Directions

Add all ingredients into the slow cooker and mix well.

Cover and cook on high for 5 hours.

Using fork shred the meat and serves.

Calories 421, Fat 16.8 g, Carbohydrates 6.2 g, Sugar 1.9 g, Protein 58.4 g, Cholesterol 169 mg

Spicy Beef Stew

Total Time: 8 hours 25 minutes

Serves: 4

Ingredients

1 lb beef stew meat
1 cup beef broth
1 onion, sliced
14.5 oz can tomatoes, diced
1 tbsp curry powder
1 fresh jalapeno pepper, diced
1 tsp fresh ginger, chopped
2 garlic cloves, minced
1 tbsp vegetable oil
Pepper
Salt

Directions

Heat oil in the pan over medium heat.

Add beef to the pan and cook until brown. Transfer to the slow cooker.

Season browned beef with pepper and salt.

In same pan, sauté ginger, garlic, and jalapeno for 2 minutes.

Add tomatoes and curry powder and stir for a minute. Transfer pan mixture to the slow cooker.

Add remaining ingredients and mix well.

Cover and cook on low for 8 hours.

Serve and enjoy.

Calories 293, Fat 11.1 g, Carbohydrates 10 g, Sugar 5 g, Protein 37.2 g, Cholesterol 101 mg

CPSIA information can be obtained
at www.ICGtesting.com
Printed in the USA
BVHW041641070221
599576BV00005B/391